A Cherokee Feast of Days

VOLUME TWO

A CHEROKEE
FEAST
OF DAYS

VOLUME TWO

Joyce Sequichie Hifler

Di Ka No He SGi-Di Go We Li SGi
(She Who Writes Her Philosophy on Paper)

COUNCIL OAK BOOKS
TULSA, OKLAHOMA

COUNCIL OAK PUBLISHING CO., INC.
TULSA, OKLAHOMA 74120

©1996 by Joyce Sequichie Hifler.
01 00 99 97 96   5 4 3 2 1

Library of Congress Card Catalog Number
91-77973
ISBN 1-57178-025-4

THE AUTHOR WISHES TO ACKNOWLEDGE with deep appreciation the help of the late Mildred Milam Viles, daughter of a Cherokee chief, who supplied American Indian quotations from her extensive library in Claremore, Oklahoma.

Portions of this work are taken from the author's nationally syndicated newspaper column, *Think on These Things*, or other names the newspapers may prefer.

The Cherokee words and phrases are phonemic translations from the Cherokee syllabary which was given to the Cherokee people about 1821 by Cherokee genius Sequoyah. Several dialects change the pronunciations.

To my husband, Charles J. Zofness
To my daughter, Jane Hifler
To my Friend and Counselor,
  The Holy Spirit

FOREWORD

ALEXANDER POPE WROTE, "Lo, the poor Indian! Whose untutored mind sees God in the clouds and hears Him in the wind."

I am an Indian. I am a Cherokee. And I see God in the clouds and I hear Him in the wind. When I was a child I thought I could hear time, and I knew what the dove and whippoorwill said when they called from the meadows and the woodland.

It is the nature of the Indian to hear with the spirit because his life is based on spiritual foundations, immovable foundations that motivate him to worship. Music is a part of this, music from rustling leaves and singing streams, but from gifted people as well. Tears came when I first heard classical music in my youth, for I was being introduced to the angels. It still happens whenever I hear strains of violin music.

Come to the table, come and feast with the Spirit, not because the Indian is good, but because the Lord is merciful.

Gv ge yu i – Love

ONE
So-Qua

COLD MONTH
Unu la ta nee'

The prairie is large and good,
and so are the heavens above,
and I do not want them stained
by the blood of war.

SATANTA
KIOWA CHIEFTAIN

January 1

Early morning sunlight sets frosted grasses ablaze with gems, topaz, emeralds, diamonds, and the heart is supremely rich, *u wa nei i*, and very enlightened.

Such mornings call us to brightness of spirit and to healing the deep hurts of the soul. Step out and breathe in the peace. Turn up the palms to give thanks and receive strength for the day and wisdom to begin this year.

Because nature thrives where humans give up, the negative is turned away. All around us the breathtaking views tell us to do the same.

You look at me and see an ugly old man, but within I am filled with great beauty.

TLO TSI HEE
OLD MAN BUFFALO GRASS
NAVAJO

3

January 2

Little quiet spells are as rare as jewels. Many can't stand even a little silence and try to fill it with empty chatter—or with words that should never have been spoken.

It is a great art to be silent. The Cherokee calls it *da lo ni ge s to di - e lu we i*, which is golden silence.

We paint with our words that which we want others to see, and we choose colors to communicate, to understand, to sense. The fewest words make silence speak most eloquently.

The fruits of silence are self-control, courage, endurance, patience and dignity.

OHIYESA
DAKOTA

January 3

Some say reality is a thing that can be touched. But reality is more real in the invisible than all we see and touch with our fingers.

Trying to face reality without knowing what it is is little different from seeing a tiny stone and finding it is a boulder buried in the earth. Reality is not a one-dimensional flat surface where everything is visible—but it is spirit and life and faith and love. We may not observe these things but we feel their influence.

Prayer is the straight line to the invisible, changing what we see from above and beneath. We cannot see it, but it is the substance of reality, the *u w wi* and *a da nv to*, heart and soul of life in its highest form.

It does not require many words to speak the truth.

CHIEF JOSEPH
NEZ PERCE

January 4

Tough-spirited, sensitive, poetic, Geronimo. Thousands could not subdue him, his freedom was too important and his life too entwined in the refuge of nature. But a time came when he wanted to surrender and live peaceably. He simply commented:

"I have to die sometime, but even if the heavens were to fall on me I want to do what is right. There is one God looking down on us all. We are all children of one God. God is listening to me. The sun, darkness, the winds are all listening to what we say."

It is in our power to say, "I hear You, and I surrender."

I am going to try to live well and peaceably.

GERONIMO
APACHE

January 5

The ground beneath our feet can seem awfully slippery at times. Something mental or emotional catches us off guard and we fall to our knees as though we are totally helpless.

Never add self-criticism to the load. This is one of the first things we try to do—blame ourselves that we could not see. Why were we not stronger? Why did our faith fail and where did the power go in a crisis?

We grieve because we think we have failed—because we could not hold the line. No, we have not failed, we have loved. We have held life softly and reverently and change has come.

Every hillside, every valley, every plain and grove, has been hallowed by some sad or happy event in days long vanished.

SEATTLE
SUQUAMISH
1786-1866

January 6

What have we of life's beautiful things? A rainbow's shimmering hues when a shower has ended? A warm brown puppy in the sunlight? A mockingbird singing while a thin veil of clouds is drawn like misty curtains across the face of the moon; a playhouse where string is stretched from tree to tree to shut out invaders; children's laughter and the fluttering of bird wings in a tiny flowing stream?

The best of beautiful things are still free. They are bits and pieces of joyful things that become a part of us—a child in a field of daisies, a friendly hand, a smile, a whispered prayer. What are we that is not a fragment from a past happiness—*a i yu quu—v hna i—to hi dv*, a moment of peace?

When we see the changes of day and night, the sun, moon, and stars in the sky, and the changing seasons upon the earth...anyone must realize that it is the work of someone more powerful than man.

CHASED-BY-BEARS
SANTEE SIOUX

8

January 7

To the Cherokee, the land is not dirt and stone and trees, it is a life-nourisher. The seed is more than a dormant embryo, it is life. The person is more than a human creature, he is a spirit.

It is never the worship of nature—but it is the love and adoration of that which set it all in motion, the Substance behind moisture, the sunlight, the rise and fall of the tides.

Incredible things are happening right before our eyes, but most are looking for things to mourn and things to celebrate. Look behind the events. The rays of sun can damage—but the reason behind all these depths and heights heals and restores.

The sun is my father; the earth is my mother; on her bosom I will repose.

TECUMSEH
SHAWNEE

January 8

Every day is a day of worship to the spiritual nature of the *Tsi la gi*. Born close to the basics, he sees "God in the clouds and hears Him in the wind," as Alexander Pope wrote. The innate greatness of it buoys him up and helps him walk in a whole new dimension.

Reasons to understand come in the simplest of things—the ice crystals touching his face are just another form of the same moisture that forms dew and snowflakes, raindrops, and even steam when under pressure. It is no mystery that the Threefold Being can be together and yet separate.

Simplicity—and yet, deep throbbing life that might not be seen with the naked eye, but is sensed all the same.

I think the Great Spirit is looking at all that is said here, and for that reason I am talking the truth.

LITTLE RAVEN
ARAPAHO LEADER

January 9

When someone slings a dart, a comment that hurts, we want to hit back. The indignity of an attack for no reason is beyond our understanding.

Persons with no conscience sling arrows without thought of where they hit. Their desire is to hit something. What we have not known is that we can turn them back. We don't have to accept everything that is said.

The quickest way to deflate the egotist is to see him as not important enough to take into account. His type of disease is contagious, and you should never expose yourself to such painful maladies.

You have compelled us to do that which makes us ashamed.

CORNPLANT
SENECA CHIEF
1781

January 10

Know that you are not the only one
to ever feel humiliation and pain. There is nothing
new under the sun. Many have been through this
valley and they understand what you are having to
bear.

Never lose faith because you asked and did
not receive. We can ask amiss, but more than likely
we are edged out by a subtle something we did not
recognize as danger.

As remote as it seems, this experience will
pass. This time and place and reason cannot be
stolen when the space is filled with praise, because
praise is giving.

*We always give the Great Spirit something. I think
that is good.*

BLACKFOOT
CROW CHIEF

January 11

People know important things about living, but too often know it with their heads and not their hearts. Heart knowledge changes a person at the core. It is important to know that it is not what goes into us that makes a difference but what comes out.

Give the heart reason to rejoice—not because of outer circumstances but from that inner source of knowing that we do not have to lie down and die because someone said it. Give the heart reason to say, "I will live and not die, I will rejoice and not cry."

My friends, I have been asked to show you my heart. I am glad to have a chance to do so.

CHIEF JOSEPH
NEZ PERCE

January 12

A wall stands between what our senses tell us and what our spirits know to be true. Our eyes, our hearing, our touch, tell us things are one way—but our circumstances tell us we need strong medicine beyond what we see and feel.

Why can't something overtake us and supply companionship and healing and money for both needs and wants? Probably because we are caught up in what we see and hear and sense, and we know too little about the spiritual.

We have two kinds of awareness—sense awareness and spiritual knowing. Intellect says we know it all. Spirit grieves for the power and gold sifting through ragged holes in our undeveloped awareness of who we are and what is available to us.

I am the maker of my own fortune...as great as the conceptions of my own mind, when I think of the spirit that rules the universe.

TECUMSEH
SHAWNEE CHIEF
12TH OF AUGUST, 1810

January 13

So few people are worthy of our tears—only a few. Our personal space is invaded and we are made to think we caused the rift that follows. This is an illusion that is not worthy of the price we try to pay.

It is the elders' privilege to look back and smile. They, too, have known the ideal, the magnificent, the ultimate—and they have cried. But *a da to li s di*, that wonderful grace, provided knowledge of how to hold one loose thread in place by joy—not tears. And then came peace.

It is the duty of the brave when injured to lay peace aside...and then to lay down again in peaceful quiet.

PUSHMATAHA
CHOCTAW CHIEF
1812

15

January 14

Many trails lead away from the right path. Our feet wander far for answers to the same questions our old ones sang about and prayed over in the quiet of their own thoughts.

Do we have new problems? No, it is the same one, *tsv s gi na*, the enemy that tries to rule our thinking and actions. He comes dressed in circumstances that will entice us to his way. But he is still the same old enemy who keeps trying.

There is nothing new under the sun. The same devils that tried the souls of ancient men have a new vulnerable generation—and not enough are aware of the danger.

From here on I want to live in peace.

GERONIMO
APACHE

January 15

The pond reflects a day of mist in gray tones. When the sky is blue, the pond is blue. Patterns like icewebs spread across the frozen surface in the middle of winter—so like we are when we take on the moods of others.

Hills and lakes and fields are touched by the actions of the sky and wind. In the night season and all through the day changes take place. Sometimes the sky glitters with wings—sometimes it is softened by snowflakes. Man's soul has a light like that of a lantern that is untroubled in the turmoil of wind and storm. But we must know what we are reflecting.

My Grandchildren, be good. Try to make a mark for yourselves. Learn all you can.

SITTING BULL
SIOUX MEDICINE MAN AND CHIEF

January 16

Use your imagination for its intended use—to create beauty and happiness and justice. If you use it for unfriendly reasons, it will eventually steal your wings and your feet. The Cherokee way of saying it is *di gu yi s gi*, the paymaster, the returns based on how it has been used. Do not envy another person, for your own imagination has grand gifts for you. Great suffering has been the lot of many who used their talented minds to bring hurt and pain where there should have been harmony.

There was nothing between him and the Big Holy. The contact was immediate and personal.

CHIEF LUTHER STANDING BEAR
LAKOTA

January 17

Tender gifts come to us all—gifts from some deep inner space that is priceless and stirs our most creative sense. A beautiful, personal revelation is like touching electricity without its harmful effects. But this is something to be kept in the heart and not talked about to others. If others have never known the touch of a shooting star nor felt the awe of being given spiritual knowledge, their response is incredulity and disbelief—which makes us question our own sanity. Protect the gift, treasure it, love it. The time will come to use it.

They are clean to a fault...they keep their stock in good order, and are hard working, painstaking people.

AGENT THOMAS JORDAN
(ABOUT THE NEZ PERCES)
SEPTEMBER 6, 1881

January 18

Talk to your body, talk to your mind, and give support to your spirit. These are your friends, your lifemates, your agility, your harmony, and your joy. Degrade them and they will fail you—not out of revenge but because it is you who keeps them in working order, who supplies them with the strength and well-being they need. Tell your legs and feet and knees how strong and steady they are, and tenderly clean the mind of trash you may have inadvertently thrown there. When something is out of order, call it back into place—and give thanks for the privilege. These are precious things, never talk negatively to them nor condemn them—because you will be condemning yourself.

The Indian thinks of places and sends his prayers there to win help and blessing.

DAKOTA WISEMAN
1800s

January 19

Rigid routine, rigid thought, can make rigid bodies. Turn off the paved path and put your foot on the earth. Feel the pulse, the life, the clean earth. If there are things that keep you from seeing the horizon, look straight up. The sky is there above the smoke, the smog, the haze that would hide the blue. Reach out and lay your fingers in the flow of any little stream—clean water is there behind the chemicals, beyond the things that would pollute. Lift your spirit above the sirens and shrill voices and ugliness of graceless personalities. Pause for even a minute in an attitude of worship. It is your day.

Each soul must meet the morning sun, the new sweet earth and the Great Silence alone.

OHIYSA
SANTEE DAKOTA

January 20

The wounded frequently want to hurt others. Meanness is not always involved but an unconscious bitterness that wants to control. The worst wounds are not always physical. Some who have suffered psychological wounds are bent on full payment whether or not it is due. The pity of it is, the wounded is the only one that cannot escape. Pain and unforgiveness are replayed day after day— as though sadness is an honorable reason never to heal. Whole lifetimes are given to demanding respect and veneration—for no other reason than life has dealt them a wound, a wound that would heal if there were a little love.

A man ought to desire that which is genuine instead of that which is artificial.

OKUTE
TETON SIOUX
1911

January 21

Identity does not require a label—for man is spirit, and spirit is nonpolitical and unconscious of color or class. An Indian woman is not as apt to board a luxury cruise ship or to sit at a bridge table hour after hour as she is to pitch camp beside some sparkling stream where the sunset tips the mountains with gold. People are different and fall naturally into different categories—though basically they are spiritual entities. These diverse spirits can even love each other if they can evade the labels. Labels are indicative of importance—but it is the heart that counts.

Is it wicked of me because my skin is red? Is it wrong of me to love my own? I am a Sioux because I was born where my father lived.

SITTING BULL
SIOUX

January 22

Words are judged by what we have in our hearts. Our ears pick up the words we hear, but once inside the heart decides the meaning.

Love is one of those words. To some it is purely physical—and others hear it as flowery springtime with little substance. But to some it is healing and a deep and wonderful commitment that cannot waver. It is the power at the core of a person, a strength not dependent on muscle and bone but life and principle and character. If the heart is right, the decision cannot fail.

I shall exercise my calm, deliberate judgment in behalf of those most dear to me...

PUSHMATAHA
CHOCTAW LEADER

January 23

We can walk through a thousand people's lives and feel only the loneliness of our own existence. Others move by on both sides and some of them stand in the brightest light while our own corner is so dark. But we have to know that the noisy successes of other people are often their ways of dealing with the still places in their lives. Others are working with their lacks and needs, their call for recognition. All of us would be warriors. All of us would stitch red into our costumes. Fear can penetrate the strongest fortress—and the password is compassion, pure and simple understanding.

The Great Spirit made us all—He made my skin red and yours white; He placed us on this earth, and intended that we should live differently from each other.

PETALESHARO
PAWNEE PRINCIPAL CHIEF

January 24

Homecoming is not just a certain hour but a feeling, an attitude, an *un na li*—a friend. One phase of the day has been completed, so now back to the reasons for it—home. Home with its familiar fragrances, its lighted warmth and peace of mind.

At least, home ought to be this way—though it isn't always. Too little time, too much weariness, too many complaints. Too little, too late, too bad. Real homecoming is a state of mind. Someone needs to be comforted, someone needs a gentle touch, someone needs to think of others. It may not be perfect, but working together makes homecoming a celebration.

Do not touch the money of the white man or his clothes. We do not fight for these things. The Seminole is fighting for his hunting grounds.

OSCEOLA
SEMINOLE WAR CHIEF

January 25

Dust trails on the ground and vapor trails in the sky where man travels with such speed we can only see where he has been—and these are everyday wonders.

Others have left tracks for us—men and women we may never have heard about, or it may be our own mothers and fathers. Eras pass leaving only the faintest signs. Hills stay pretty much the same, the sky changes and changes again. The wind sweeps a trail of seeds that give us trees and flowers. Universal tracks—footsteps we hear again and again. Will ours be marching—or rolling softly as the steps of an evening walker?

I thank the Great Spirit for making me a Sauk, and the son of a great Sauk Chief.

BLACK HAWK

January 26

Peace at any price is not peace, it is hiding until the danger passes. Sooner or later those who have no honor will find another way to break the treaty.

Tread water when necessary, avoid confrontation with those who love turmoil, and never be so self-sufficient as to not be able to say an honest prayer when it is needed. Cultivate peace, *to hi dv*, but do not give in to darkness.

Take away your guns and swords, the cause of all our jealousy, or you may die in the same manner.

WHAHUNSONACOCK
POWHATAN
1600

January 27

Trust is a fragile gem that most people never intend to lose. Too often a promise is easily made and easily broken. It reveals a deeper nature that may never have been trustworthy. A Cherokee elder once commented, "Indian may forgive—but Indian never forget." No grudge, but wisdom that a trust shattered one time may well be broken again.

Trust is a stand—*a ga to gv*—says the Cherokee. If the Spirit is trustworthy, then we should be truthworthy. He is the Gem, the Power of the stand we take. We personally have no power—but the Gem has it all.

The Indian world was devoted to living; the European world to getting.

HISTORIAN
1764

January 28

Losing is not always what it seems, and how we react makes the difference. We may be disappointed, feel let down—and maybe a little betrayed—but we haven't lost until we quit.

What is done is done. We have cried and we have hurt—but this will show the stuff we are made of and how nothing can keep us down. How we think, what we say, and where we put our faith will set our new course and keep us on it.

Our new home will be beyond a great river on the way to the setting sun . . . our wigwams on another land where we hope the Great Spirit will smile upon us.

KEOKUK
SAUK LEADER
1832

January 29

An individual responsibility is to set the course of the day, a year—a lifetime. Words and thoughts bring us to some crucial point of strength or else utter weakness.

Decide now to forgive. It does not mean reconciling with an enemy—but it does mean freedom. Decide to love—others, but yourself in particular. Wait until the flames settle before you take on the problem. Even tempers and orderly minds can handle heat better. Walk softly, for others are on the same road and they look for a gentle word, less criticism and full observance of the Spirit.

We, the people composing the Eastern and Western Cherokee Nation...by virtue of our original and inalienable rights, do hereby solemnly and mutually agree . . . to one body politic . . . the Cherokee Nation.

SEQUOYAH
CHEROKEE LEADER

January 30

Nothing is sweeter than to have a friend to rely on. We need each other to ease worry, to give and get reassurance. But when that reliance focuses on nothing but problems, then there needs to be a change toward solutions.

Problems can make some people feel significant. The struggle can be too important and having someone hear all about it can detract from friendship. We can never do another person a greater service than to stop being a prop for unstable emotions. Love and care and support—but never be a prop. It steals the floor where a person needs to stand.

The Cherokee people do not desire to be involved in war, but self-preservation fully justifies them to the course they have adopted and they will be recreant to themselves if they do not sustain it.

JOHN ROSS
CHIEF, CHEROKEE NATION

January 31

Something to look forward to gives us reason to get up in the morning. It may be no more than watching the sun lay long shadows across the land, or enjoying the aroma of coffee and the sound of bacon sizzling in the skillet.

Life's little pleasures give us greater compassion and the ability to comfort and to be comforted. It is a lonely road that does not have time for the daily joys that are so common but so enlivening.

Certain small things and observances sometimes have connection with large and more profound ideas.

PLENTY-COUPS
CROW NATION

TWO
(Ta-li)

BONY MONTH
Gaga lu'nee

We do not want riches but we do want to train our children right. Riches would do us no good. We could not take them with us to the other world. We do not want riches, we want peace and love.

RED CLOUD
SIOUX CHIEFTAIN

February 1

*G*a sa qua lv, the circle, infinite life in its cycling process—inhaling and exhaling. The sun draws moisture from the earth and disperses it back to us in a continual movement around the clock called life. We are on the journey of giving and receiving.

Father-Creator knew we would not be self-sufficient and gave us willing hands and loving hearts with which to give and to receive. Look up, the sun and moon and stars are all round and travel in cycles. Our cycle should be the most beautiful of all—for we are life and spirit.

Even the seasons form a great circle in their changing, and always come back again to where they were.

HEHAKA SAPA
OGLALA
1800s

February 2

A walk down a country road in memory is almost as good now as when it happened—and even better at times. The youthful urgency to skip some of life's steps is replaced with patience and endurance, and even amusement.

Getting there was utmost and now we know that "there" is a place in the heart—not a place where all wishes are granted. A song and a prayer in the heart are worth all the visual triumphs in the world. A deep down harmony and spiritual joy erases all that was not quite right. American Indians call this new consciousness, "walking in a sacred manner."

The warriors sat in a circle waiting on the Holy Man and he came forth singing a holy song . . .

SHORT BULL
DAKOTA SIOUX

February 3

If it is going to offend you, don't look and don't listen. Offense is a weapon used against peaceable people. It tries to keep us from seeing the morning sun and feeling the mist against our faces.

Everything tries to tamper with happiness—and happiness is not because of something but in spite of something. Don't be receptive to ugliness designed to amuse—or to inform, as some so cleverly put it. Offense leaves a wound that has trouble healing.

All miserable as we seem in your eyes, we consider ourselves much happier than you.

MICMAC CHIEF
1676

February 4

It is a blessing that we need each other. Communication brings vitality and energy and lovely sharing. This does not mean we say the same things or eat the same food and think the same thoughts. It means we share space without rancor and envy. It means we are happy to see each other in good health and doing well.

A Cherokee grandmother advises, "Celebrate being an individual. It is a good time to be one's own best friend—and it is time to unfold one's spirit to draw in someone less secure."

I fear no man, and I depend only upon the Great Spirit.

ADARIO
HURON
1600s

February 5

What sort of persons are we—and what discipline do we obey? Have we slipped the responsibility of inner law and must we depend on outer man-made rules to stay in line?

Every one of us needs a Prompter that lives in the heart and rules the affairs with love and peace and stability. A free-flowing spirit is needed to tell us where the limits are—and what things are right and which will damage and destroy.

Control for our minds and bodies is in our power, and with it peace and contentment. When these two things begin to fade, we know we have begun to lean on others to tell us who we are and what we can do.

You depend upon an infinity of persons whose places have raised them above you. Is it true or not?

KONDIARONK
HURON CHIEF

February 6

The danger of wielding a big stick is that it can so easily turn on you.

An unwritten law dictates the total downfall of any person or group of persons whose aim it is to manipulate and overrun other people. This is not to say it can't be done. It is done all the time by intimidation and sarcasm. But nothing lasts that comes through overbearing force.

The underlying principle must be considered in every phase of living. It is the equalizer, the balancing factor that says if we plan to sink someone else's ship, we had better be good swimmers.

You can count your money . . . but only the Great Spirit can count the grains of sand.

CHIEF
BLACKFEET TRIBE

February 7

We blame far too much on age and too little on attitudes. Life is meant to be lived without dreading birthdays or looking for signs that one's natural force is abated.

Life is meant to be lived for a good reason—to tell the negative forces we will not be defeated. We will not be a royal pain nor roam through life without a purpose. Each of us has a purpose and we will not give it up until the course is finished.

When someone asks, "How are you?" answer, "Well to do, *wa du*—thank you!"

What is life? It is the flash of a firefly in the night . . . it is the little shadow which runs across the grass and loses itself in the sunset.

CROWFOOT
BLACKFOOT
1877

February 8

Spirit has no high blood pressure. Spirit has no pressure of any kind. Look up at the leaves moving at the top of the tallest tree. No man has ever touched those leaves—but Spirit has. Look at the puffy clouds scudding across the sky—and catch the scent of evergreen—so many things set in motion by Spirit.

Answers to questions may be out of reach—but not the Spirit. Send out your invisible praisers and singers to set the pace, to enlighten your spirit. When the blessing comes—ask. The Spirit knows.

I know how hard it is for youth to listen to the voice of age.

WASHAKIE
SHOSHONE
1870

February 9

Like the haystacks of youth, life has its hidden tunnels that are dark and exciting and full of adventure. We have been warned that there is danger that the hay could collapse and could bury us alive. But not us, we are invincible. We know enough to get out before the collapse comes.

Will there be anyone there to dig us out the way a farmer had to free his cows before they suffocated? The cows ate straight through the hay without knowing there was danger. We have been eating straight through—and when guilt says to stop it—our craving, our sense of adventure says, "After this."

I shall go a little farther, and then a little farther, until I get so far away as is possible for me.

KICKING BIRD
CROW
1865

February 10

Great people from over the years have known the wisdom of taking time to set their minds adrift. They seem to sit idly on the side-lines—but they are really fishing in their minds for solutions rather than thinking only about problems.

Creative work has always resulted from silent and deep thought. Physical weariness will disappear when the mind is allowed to ramble and rest.

Knowledge comes from study and observation, but wisdom comes in the quiet times—and particularly when time is made for a *da nv to—u ga na s dv* which means "the sweet Spirit."

The ground says, "It is the Great Spirit that placed me here."

YOUNG CHIEF
CAYUSE
1855

February 11

Success, in part, depends on staying power. What seems to be a remarkable idea on paper may be a colossal failure in practice. This is why we have to have more to us than just what shows.

Whether we are building a house or a business, a bridge or a life, we have to have something to back it up. Most losses result from investing in what looks good but has no substance, a flash in the pan that dies as suddenly as it began. The strength of anything is to know it, to give it strong moral character—and to decide there is a principle to be kept.

Great Spirit sees and hears everything, and he never forgets.

IN-MUT-TOO-YAH-LAT-LAT
NEZ PERCE

February 12

Beauty and ugliness are everywhere—even in some of the same things. To some a wide-open prairie is empty and colorless—but to others it is uncluttered simplicity—the way life itself ought to look.

Physical appeal is high on some lists, but *nu tso se dv na*, which is Cherokee comfort, lasts longer. Whatever is in our hearts is in our sight. To love something or someone makes us see the beauty of it—not the wrong.

It is to our advantage to be gentle in our observations—to see and cultivate the best in who we are and in those around us.

We love quiet; we suffer the mouse to play; when the woods are rustled by the wind, we fear not.

INDIAN CHIEF
1796

February 13

Ninety percent of what we worry and talk about never happens. If it were not for fear, insurance companies would go broke overnight and all the energy we pack into talking would be put into getting well and becoming wealthy.

Many exquisite rewards exist for those of us who can stop talking trouble. If we could keep our mouths shut and our eyes and ears open, there would be far fewer things to prey on us.

The armies of the whites are without number, like the sands of the sea, and ruin will follow all tribes that go to war with them.

SHABONEE
POTAWATOMI

February 14

The things that try people's souls are not always from outside themselves. Fear is one of those things and it has no right to intrude on our peace of mind. But it will if we let it.

We are weakened when we tell ourselves we cannot help what we feel. Feelings are like the pounding of the surf that washes over things that are supposed to be permanent. Sandbag them!

We are wise and strong when we say we are—and we are well and happy when we dwell on being well and happy instead of hearing all the things that "could be." Everyone is trying to get ahead by being forewarned—but your spirit knows what is true. Let it warn you.

Give him to us and we promise you he shall never lie again.

TESSOUAT
OTTAWA CHIEF

February 15

Like children, slender new oaks have taken a stand beneath the great ones that have stood the seasonal changes for well over a hundred years. What stories they could tell about the wild animals and human creatures that have shared this place.

These spreading oaks have a blush of green haloed in early morning rays, and on cloudy days a mist hangs like gauzy curtains to blue the shadows. Here the wild rose canes have turned from green to gray and back to green many many times.

What man is does not always show on the face he wears—but this wood has no masks. Its comforting arms invite us to love and share and to feel at home.

As I stand before you my mind runs over many fierce battles...but now my heart is glad.

KOON-KAH-ZA-CHY
APACHE CHIEF

February 16

Virginia creeper spreads through the lush compost of the woods like veins in soft skin and climbs through the rough bark of the post oak to the very top.

We weave through the rough places trying to reach the top because we feel some ungrateful god has put this on us to deal with—to somehow teach us. But such feelings are false.

How many times has the creeper been snagged and pulled from its growing place—as often as we are delayed in reaching our goals. What are we, helpless victims trying to overcome, or hardy individuals that will not be beaten? Attitude, all attitude.

I was going around the world with the clouds and air, when God spoke to my thought and told me to come in here and be at peace with all.

COCHISE
APACHE LEADER

February 17

Listen for wisdom and instruction. If you do not, it will pass by the way a deer moves soundlessly over the woodland path. Listen for the inner voice that will never be the source of anything wrong.

Listen to how you use your own words. Words are seeds that plant a living garden or they are seeds that sprout weeds that are invasive.

Stop being down on yourself. No human being is perfect—least of all those who believe they are. Give yourself credit for what you have done right, and, even though that may seem like a miracle, you can do it again.

He [the president] can sit in his town and drink his wine, while you [Governor Harrison] and I will fight it out.

TECUMSEH
SHAWNEE

February 18

Walk away for a minute. Stop listening to the hard luck stories, because as concerned as you are, it is no good if you sink out of sight.

Rest. Let it all go, because mind, body, and spirit all need a quiet place. If the spirit is in the right place, the body can rest more deeply.

Taking care is a personal responsibility. No one else is going to do it for you—because no one can. If there is anything good to think about, if there is anything to dwell on that is joyful, then think on these things. Give it time and see it work.

We meet as brothers that have been away from each other many years.

TIN-TIN-MEET-SA
UMATILLA CHIEF

February 19

Though opportunity sometimes has flashing lights and ringing bells, wisdom comes on soft shoes. Opportunity is no good without wisdom. It sees the chance to do something but wisdom knows why and when and how.

Personality and the opportunity to perform is a part of every venture. But it takes more than a sparkling show window full of inviting merchandise. It takes staying power and quiet wisdom—and the ability to blend the two.

There need be no trouble. Treat all men alike . . . give them the same law . . . give them an even chance.

CHIEF JOSEPH
NEZ PERCE
1879

February 20

A miracle is an event beyond human power to understand—so much so that most people will shove aside the thought as unreal.

Miracles happen every day to the most common of us and at any hour. We tend to call them by a more acceptable name—coincidence. But most of these supernatural events move in like the dawn creeping across the land. It is so gradual it seems that it has always been.

What triggers a miracle? It is not outward, but something that throws a switch within. It is an event over and above anything we can explain—and why should we need to?

Day and night cannot dwell together.

SEATTLE
CHIEF, SUQUAMISH & DUWAMISH

February 21

King Solomon said that where the tree falls, there it lies. It is done, and we will not raise it up again. But it is what we do from this point forward that makes the difference.

Something that seemed so sure turns questionable, and something for which we had little hope suddenly works out. Regardless of how things appear, they can be totally different—and it is what we do from now on that will make or break us. Moving on does not mean we do not care, it means we will not let it keep us from living fully.

Tribe follows tribe, and nation follows nation, like the waves of the sea. It is the order of nature, and regret is useless.

SEATTLE
SUQUAMISH

February 22

Eager expectation is the activity of the spirit; it doesn't come from some outer excitement. Enjoy friends and don't criticize—however much the need seems to arise.

Spend time with friends and family but save some time to be alone. Peace and hope come to those who wait for them—and joy overtakes the grateful one. Even to withdraw for ten minutes breaks into the emotions to smooth away sharpness.

Be a good friend to yourself and the sweetness of it will draw others like nectar lures the honey-bee. Open your spiritual eyes and see that you are never alone.

Do not take up the warpath without a just cause and honest purpose.

PUSHMATAHA
CHOCTAW LEADER

February 23

Late on a snowy winter's evening the woods are quiet as though a woolen blanket has been laid over everything to muffle the sound. The sunset lights the western sky with wispy clouds like horsetails.

Pink and orange and purple streak the sky and slide down to glowing embers along the horizon. A thin spiral of blue smoke rises from a chimney and the sun's reflection bronzes all the windows.

It is suppertime. It is the end of the day and time to be peaceful. Grievances and unhappiness can go by the wayside and let companionship come in. It is suppertime—a time reserved for sharing the best. A pot of soup, a loaf of bread, and peace.

The many moons and sunny days we have lived here will long be remembered by us.

KEOKUK
SAUK LEADER
1780

February 24

Let us walk down the lane a little way to where the woods begin. There is not much activity here on a cold winter day, but the quiet and solitude are beautiful and comforting.

The silence will be short-lived because spring is working beneath the crusty ground. In a few weeks animals will be coming out of hibernation and the birds will be migrating.

Now is the time to enjoy the last of winter's activities. There will be more cold and more snow, but it doesn't last as long and spring beckons with beautiful suggestions of color and mellow days.

Earlier than the sun appears upon the hills, he gives thanks for his protection during the night.

CORNPLANT
SENECA CHIEF
1791

February 25

Grandmother was the matriarch—a woman of few words and a lot of action. Children and adults knew she was the driving force. She did not beg for results, she expected them.

The Cherokee family recognizes age, respects the authority of one who has lived many experiences and does not want to explain them. Her actions were not always appreciated, but there was order in the family and a learning that was to be our guide.

When adults are not wise in their love and discipline, the child must use his own inner voice of authority to keep himself disciplined. No matter how many sources of discipline, the best comes from that inner source.

In my early days I was eager to learn and do things, and therefore I learned quickly.

SITTING BULL
SIOUX
1800s

February 26

It is frequently not the opportunity we need but the lesson we must learn from having lost it. Our senses may be sharpened that timing is very important and that we have to be ready when opportunity comes.

But opportunity is still not the whole thing. Making ourselves aware, being sensitive when we brush against the chance to do something worthwhile. If we are dull of spirit then nothing beckons to us, because it couldn't get our attention if it did. Like attracts like. There must be something in us that hears the music of the spheres when everyone else says it is absolutely silent.

Did you know that trees talk? Well they do. They talk to each other, and they'll talk to you if you listen.

WALKING BUFFALO
STONEY
1800s

62

February 27

Winter storms affect things of nature the same way human storms affect us. Differences are forgotten when the problem is a common one.

Meadowlarks and doves that usually keep to the open fields come down to feed with the cardinal and titmouse. Finches and bluejays, though very different in size and temperament, feed together peaceably. The food is there in one spot and there is little dissension about who sits at the table.

If they serve no other purpose, strenuous times are great equalizers. They put people on a common basis with a common issue—to make it through. Where people survive together there is a bond of understanding. They learn to support and to look out for each other.

In my youthful days, I have seen large herds of buffalo . . . and elk in every grove, but they are here no more . . . all having gone toward the setting sun.

SHABONEE
POTAWATOMI PEACE CHIEF
1700s

February 28

We can't always gear our lives to the desires of others. And that doesn't mean we should be difficult or hard to get along with. It does mean there is a time to make it easy on ourselves.

Take a few easy steps. When life crowds in, it is time to quit giving the impression of being superhuman. Going the extra mile has always been important, but we have days when someone else needs to go that extra mile and give us relief.

It is somewhat like breathing—there's a time to inhale and a time to exhale.

You hear of us as murderers and thieves. We are not so. If we had more lands to give you, we would give them, but we have no more.

RED CLOUD
SIOUX CHIEFTAIN

THREE
Tsa'l

WINDY MONTH
Unu'la hee

We throw ourselves under the protection of the Great Spirit above . . . we wish for peace and whenever we hear that pleasant sound, we will pay attention to it.

JOSEPH BRANT,
A BRILLIANT MOHAWK
LEADER

March 1

When we stop to think, we realize that at one time our main teaching was to be honorable and just and compassionate. And now, most of our entertainment is watching someone bring down someone with a degree of innocence.

We are free to hiss and boo what we see and hear, but how many admire such a gift of treachery? What would it be like to manipulate and generally ruin other people's lives for pure entertainment?

Who can we really trust or rely on? We can begin with ourselves. By weeding out past experience and by forgiving ourselves, we can be someone that can be trusted. It is a beginning—and a responsibility.

My children, you have forgotten the customs and traditions of your forefathers.

PONTIAC
ODOWA
1763

March 2

Certain people affect us like a tight shoe that rubs in all the wrong places. We try to ignore it until we can get to a private place where we can get rid of it. But while we are wearing it the pain goes on and becomes nearly impossible to bear.

So much pecks away at us like dripping water until we cannot ignore it. In retrospect we see the foolishness of not handling the problem more quickly—but we were taught to *ha tse s da*, grin and bear it. Be nice. Be kind. But the shoe pinches and rubs and our patience grows short. How much wiser to quietly step out of the shoes and never go back.

I kept out of all the fights and troubles.

LITTLE RAVEN
ARAPAHO
1800s

March 3

Some mysteries have never been explained: how a firefly lights up its tail, how a bumblebee flies, and how a hummingbird can hover and dart.

Even deeper mysteries surround us personally. How did we get to this place to do this thing? We know little more about ourselves than we do about the firefly and the bumblebee.

To think and ponder and question is a part of our nature—but if we were to put to work what we already know we would be financial geniuses and spiritual giants. No mystery stands out here, but think what we could do were we to work like the ant—and with no overseer.

He did not depend altogether on his eyes for information.

SAID ABOUT PONTIAC
OTTAWA
1700s

March 4

An amusing story is told about Tecumseh to show how kindly tolerant he was. One evening on entering the home of a white man with whom he was friends, he saw a gigantic stranger there who was badly frightened at the sight of Tecumseh. The man for all his size took cover behind others in the room. Tecumseh stood a moment sternly watching the great fellow, and then he went up and patted the cowering giant and said good naturedly, "Big baby; big baby!"

The Great Spirit told me to tell the Indians that he had made them, and made the world—and he had placed them on it to do good and not evil.

TENSKWATAWA
1808

March 5

Once you hear the cries of geese in flight, you never forget it. Distance may muffle the sound at first—but then all is silent and that clear spirited call comes through.

The sound of geese is one of the earliest signs that the season is changing. Long ribbons pulled along in v-shape, turning like silver flecks in the sunlight before they fade into the blue.

Like other treasures we want to preserve, we need to provide a place for them as an invitation to come and awaken us with their primitive cries.

Such nearness to nature as I have described keeps the spirit sensitive to impressions not commonly felt, and in touch with unseen powers.

OHIYESA
SANTEE DAKOTA
1862

March 6

To live by one's feelings is to wilt at the first sign of opposition. Feelings are driven by the emotions and they keep us forever on unstable ground.

When we falter we are taken back immediately to a time when things didn't work out. If what we consider a failure is still reminding us years later, then it is a stumbling block that should be removed. Let the weak say, "I am strong." And let that strength rise like the phoenix out of the ashes to overcome every weak emotion.

Although wrongs have been done me I live in hopes.

BLACK KETTLE
CHEYENNE

March 7

Never underestimate the power of quiet determination. It changes the most severe circumstances and holds the line against impossible odds. It is the handle by which we make or break our lives.

Nothing can stand against quiet determination. When we decide to be well, we will be well. When we decide to prosper, we will prosper. Something as simple as the way the sun sifts through misty leaves, or the quavery call of the screech owl, erases all time but the primitive. Something happens to change all sense of proportion and things slip into their rightful pattern.

We saw the Great Spirit's work in almost everything: sun, moon, trees, wind, and mountains.

TATANGA MANI
STONEY INDIAN

March 8

It staggers the imagination to believe we can influence the direction of our lives. But we do it day after day. Every word we speak, everything we believe, builds our consciousness and makes us who we are.

If we never expect anything good, it will oblige us by going to someone who does believe in it. What others are doing matters little when we begin to see that we are as unlimited as we say we are. It is in our power to make the difference.

Each soul must meet the morning sun, the new sweet earth and the Great Silence alone.

OHIYESA
SANTEE DAKOTA

March 9

The reason those we love have so much more power to hurt us is because we are open to them. When we trust in full confidence we are without the usual protection we keep around us for those we do not trust.

Never accept words meant to hurt. Turn them back because they are the responsibility of the speaker. When you are caught off guard, hold the emotions in silence for a moment and tell them to be still. It takes longer to forget than it does to forgive—and time heals when we give it the power.

The war did not spring up here . . . the war was brought here . . .

SPOTTED TAIL
BRULÉ SIOUX

March 10

He had a face that some would say only a mother could love. Long scruffy hair and great ears that old Indians seem to grow later in life. His mouth ran from ear to ear and his nose was sufficient.

What a homely face—and why was it so sad? It makes a person wonder what thing happened to bring the tears that seem imminent. He sat quietly as though waiting for time to pass and for things to get better.

But three small ones came running and shouting, "Grandfather!" Their bony knees and elbows took him over totally and there was nothing left but joy. Shoulders straightened, eyes twinkled, lips revealed strong white teeth, and happiness took away the years. And so it is with love—the miracle of love.

Kinship with all creatures of the earth, sky and water was a real and active principle.

LUTHER STANDING BEAR
LAKOTA
1898

March 11

Our perspective sets on us some days like a jaunty hat—a little askew and not right on target. Such hats make our world out of step—everyone else is off on the wrong foot.

These are the times we should pull in our feathers and be very small and unimportant. Wrong may arise from the other side—but why get mixed up in it? This is our little space for which we are responsible and what we see, what we think, and what we say will show what kind of job we are doing.

Why don't you talk, and go straight, and let all be well?

MOTABATO
SOUTHERN CHEYENNE
1866

March 12

Lichen and sedum are greening along the edge of the woods—a clear sign of spring warming. Wild onions and purple violets edge the fallen logs and moist undergrowth.

Attitudes and health improve generously when there is such newness. The grays have faded, the bluejay and cardinal give us color in the evergreen. Birdsong fills all the space in the woods and we know the Spirit is blessing us as well. It is spring whose name is beauty.

When I was ten years of age I looked at the land and the rivers, the sky above, and the animals around me and could not fail to realize that they were made by some great power.

TATANKA-OHITIKA
SIOUX
1911

March 13

We go to meet life with our measuring cups—so much for health, so much for wealth, so much for contentment. But sometimes we do not realize we have our hand over the opening and nothing can get in.

The *u wo yi* is the hand that is controlled by the mind—the mind that asks what we deserve, and how much is possible. Hasn't this clan always been in need and not well? How can we expect to be any different? Because we can think and speak and pray. And best of all we can break the chains that have held generations in poverty and poor health. It can be done, and it should be done.

Everything as it moves, now and then, here and there, makes stops.

DAKOTA WISEMAN
1800s

March 14

Thinking and talking are so basic to us that we do not realize how they shape our lives. Thought and speech are to us what the hoe and rainfall are to the gardener. We plant a word-seed and cultivate it with our thought.

Our minds and words have to be weeded just as a garden must be cleaned. When a weed is removed there is room for a flower, room for conversation and shared thought that will reseed and bloom until the garden is beautiful. And so we become.

The earth and myself are of one mind.

CHIEF JOSEPH
NEZ PERCE

March 15

When a child is learning to walk, he falls and gets up to try again. If he were to stop getting up, he would never learn to walk. His effort not only teaches him to walk but to run and skip and do many other things as well.

All of us are learning to walk in some area. We fall down and wonder if it's worth getting up again. But we never really fail until we give up. One of the lessons we learn is that only those who are trying ever make it. We can't let go, for someone is watching us and learning courage to do the impossible.

When the sun goes down, he opens his heart before his God.

CORNPLANT
SENECA CHIEF

March 16

So much is taken for granted that it is a wonder we ever enjoy anything in its present state. While we are off chasing causes and things that look good, our nearest and dearest have no attention.

Few things necessary to us come through loud and clear. They become so much a part of us that we forget they exist—like the leg that supports us and the hand that feeds us. It is inane to gamble with such priceless assets. We should not wait any longer to speak and act with our hearts.

We must let you know we love our children too well to send them such a great way. Our customs are different from yours and you will be so good as to excuse us.

CANANSSATEGO

March 17

These are times that produce tension on every side. We are sensitive to every abrasive remark—real or imagined. We know we can neither wisely withdraw from everything nor continue the way we are.

Then it is a matter of finding the center of our spiritual lives. Nothing so becomes us as stillness and quiet serenity. A proverb says, "Her ways are ways of pleasantness, and her paths are peace." But not outwardly at first. Time and prayer will relieve the pressure—and then comes peace.

When Usen created Apaches . . . He taught them where to find the herbs, and how to prepare them for medicine.

GERONIMO
APACHE

March 18

Don't give up. We have been up against stone walls before and had no one to tell us what to do. Stay away from self-condemnation. It is designed to tear down our interest and vision. When a person loses interest, he loses his ability to see solutions.

Be quiet. Excess noise, too much talk, and too little rest only adds to the confusion. Most likely something will whisper to use reason—whose reason? The wrong reason may be the cause of most of our trouble. And that wrong reason may have come because we did not first ask *Asga Ya Galun lati*—the One who knows.

May the Lord bring you out of all your troubles. Trust your course with Him.

JOHN ROSS
CHEROKEE CHIEF

March 19

We need something to stoke our fire, to stir us into action. If we sit all day and wonder why life is passing us by, it is probably because we gave so little enthusiasm.

Lack of enthusiasm can be the result of fear—fear of disappointment, fear of what others will think or say. But on the other hand, who cares what someone might say? That is their problem, not ours.

It may seem easier not to count on anything, but if we take the time to study a situation to see what we can do, it could be worth a few disappointments to just see our own grit and enthusiasm to tackle it.

We have borne everything patiently for this long time.

JOSEPH BRANT
MOHAWK

March 20

Few people go through life without some kind of trauma. But everyone doesn't react the same way. Certain experiences are magnified by pain and kept alive by distressed memory—so hostile conditioning is the result. Our own included.

Nothing is ever fixed by glossing it over or covering it up. We cannot change what has already happened, but we can lessen the effect by putting it in perspective. It happened, it hurt, it still hurts. Talking about it makes it more vivid—but writing it in a personal journal takes it out of us and puts it somewhere else. Seeing it in black and white brings it into focus—and ultimately helps heal our wounds.

Our eyes are opened so that we see clearly.

RED JACKET
SENECA
1700s

March 21

When time passes and nothing seems to change, we are afraid that we are caught in a whirlpool that takes us around and around and goes nowhere. We don't want to be pressed into a mold that keeps us from moving forward.

Within us is the power to move mountains. Frustration and confusion can glaze that power so we become negative—but we are powerhouses, and we can break through. We are children of Light and we cannot be held against our will.

The Tsa la gi [Cherokee] does not desire to be involved in war.

JOHN ROSS
CHEROKEE CHIEF

March 22

After all the tears, spring has burst into laughter and promises of riotous color. The breezes stir the meadows as though a gentle hand brushes lilac velvet.

Birdsong overflows the woods and kittens romp among the irises and daylilies. Every day a new plant pushes through mellow earth and butterflies come in like flying flowers. Life moves outside and shows off with shameless drama. It is spring! Our hearts rejoice and our spirits sing for having this lovely experience.

The old people came literally to love the earth . . . to remove their moccasins and walk with bare feet on the sacred earth.

LUTHER STANDING BEAR
LAKOTA CHIEF

March 23

Long earrings made of turquoise and silver swung from her rather large earlobes. More silver and turquoise lay on her bosom and on her wrists and long brown fingers. She was lacing leather in soft moccasins as she watched a much older man having difficulty walking on rough ground.

"Be careful," she said, "what you watch others doing. If you see yourself at his age and having his problems, then change your view. You haven't had his hardships, you probably won't even live to be as old as he is, and now is when you should correct what is wrong."

Aunts, mothers, and grandmothers teach. Can we hear?

Our relations with the neighboring tribes are of the most friendly character. Let us see that the white path which leads from our country to theirs be obstructed by no act of ours.

JOHN ROSS
CHEROKEE CHIEF

March 24

At the close of day when owls call to each other in the woods, we say, "There's Grandfather." Not grandfather owl but Grandfather Sequichie. He could mimic an owl so well that another owl would answer.

As children fishing with him on the creek bank at night, we worried that there might be an owl revolt when so many came close to our campfire and called to this talented Indian. What would they do when they found out they had been fooled?

His attention was diverted to a fish on the line and he forgot to keep calling and the owls at last drifted away. It was comforting to feel the still warm dust on the road home and know we had escaped another owl attack.

I think to come and visit you tomorrow, and to talk over many things that I have seen in my journey.

TEEDYUSCUNG
DELAWARE
1758

March 25

Know that reason gets away from people in the heat of the moment and they do things that are totally without reason. Just stop worrying about what other people will think and do what is necessary for protection.

If you live in fear, pray for help—and then go meet it. Never wait for miracles—cause some. And it will amaze you how others understand and give you support.

Life needs a mind-renewal, but sometimes we can't wait for that process. The time to move is when darkness hovers. This is the time to stop wavering. This is your hour, take it.

Hardly any two...agree on what should be done.

SPOTTED TAIL
LAKOTA
CIRCA 1880

March 26

The end of the day brings out the emotions. Some come alive at the first sign of dusk, and evening softness suggests things to be—and things that never were.

And then there is night—a time when bone-tiredness can make a pillow heaven until some bit of worry begins to tap on the consciousness. Night, like the tongue, magnifies, and everything is bigger than life.

But morning comes—and with it the realization of what is finished and what there is left to do. If night has not done its work well, then day has to call the shots—and the sooner the better. This day does not belong to stress. I will call it peace.

You told us to speak our minds freely. We now do it.

LITTLE TURTLE
MIAMI
1795

March 27

Things have been shaky before, and some things broke down—but with courage we made it. We made it because we decided to stand up and not let anything whip us.

The best revenge against anything that would tear us apart is to not let it happen. We simply have to see things for what they really are. It will pass. And if we do not grieve and blame ourselves we will overcome every memory, every wound, and flow in strength and security. Just a little courage— and a big decision to use it.

It is a white man's treaty, and the white man did not make the Indian understand it as he meant it.

MICANOPY
SEMINOLE

March 28

Worry about how much we can remember can throw the mind into such stress that it cannot function right. The harder we try, the less we are going to recall.

As living progresses there is more to remember, and very little of it worthy fact. The incessant chatter that goes on around us is not important and when it comes to the children's ages—let them remember.

If there is something we really want to retain, then we should write it down. A notebook has saved many a day and acts as a companion to someone who doesn't want to remember everything.

We love the Great Spirit—we acknowledge his supreme power—our peace, our health, and our happiness depend upon him.

PETALESHARO
PAWNEE
1822

March 29

What we say reaches far. Someone is listening for hope, someone is reaching for help—and it may be us. What do we need to hear? Say it for others. When we say it, we hear it as well. We hear it twice, through our ears and through our hearts.

Children and pets and older people need the voice of love and common sense. They long for the happy voice, the tone that says all is well and there is no danger. Lord, we all need to hear peace so much—and there is so little spoken.

We looked up to the Great Spirit. We went to our Father. We were encouraged.

BLACK HAWK
SAC
1832

March 30

This morning cool breezes blew up from the river bottom and stirred the new green leaves on the pin oak. The change of season wavers from cool brisk air to warm pockets trapped beneath heavy foliage.

We, too, waver because of changes that tell us something is pending. Something is adjusting the days and hours, and we can't seem to pin it down.

The deer lifts its head to catch a scent—should it be afraid? As creatures with spirits, we do the same things—testing and sniffing the breeze to detect anything different. Are we ready?

The Cherokee removal was the cruelest work I have ever known.

JAMES MOONEY
RECORDING CHEROKEE HISTORY
CIRCA 1835

March 31

Real power is often just knowing when to keep our mouths shut. We have so much we want to say and so many to say it to that it is almost impossible to stay silent.

But silence teaches in a way that nothing else can. The mind makes deep adjustments in the quiet times. True laughter bubbles up from humor too precious for words—and brings with it a joy that dissolves disappointment.

Real, mind-changing power is of the spirit and can clear a path a mile wide through pain. The human spirit fights valiantly, and when it is blended with this power, it comes out like a tiger.

My heart is big and glad that you have told us that you will not make war on Indians.

KICKING BIRD
KIOWA
1800s

FOUR
Nun ki'

FLOWER MONTH
Tsi law 'nee

The Great Spirit made the Indians to be a single people, quite distinct from white men and for different purposes.

TENSKWATAWA
SHAWNEE PROPHET

April 1

April! Golden girl of the year, clad in the newest shade of green with meadow skirts strewn with every color and cradling nests of baby birds close to your breast.

Your jewels sparkle in the morning mist, long strands of dew drops draping the fence rows and turning to emeralds and rubies in early morning light.

Tears come easily but you are often laughing as you move through a range of temperatures that gives the human spirit reason to celebrate. You are adored, sweet girl of spring, for life the way you serve it.

My heart is filled with joy when I see you here, as the brooks fill with water when the snow melts in spring.

PARRA-WA-SAMEN
COMANCHE
1867

April 2

Most of our thought runs to what we do not have and to what we are not apt to get. Those are fear thoughts and reminders of how we let our minds get on the wrong path. But how can a person have faith in a world so out of focus?

Don't self-sabotage. Don't become your own worst enemy. Don't stay ignorant, and do shed labels. Do think beyond the right to be a certain way. If something is destroying you, be smart and get rid of it. And remember that intellectual preaching is not worth dirt if we have failed to meditate on the right words.

The Comanches are not blind like the pups of the dog when seven sleeps old.

TEN BEARS
COMANCHE

April 3

A walk in the silent woods is not silent at all. Stand still and listen. The thump of a downy woodpecker on a hollow log, the tiny hooves of a deer scooting through last season's leaves, and best of all, the soft rumble of thunder and the spatter of drops on the broad leaf of the hickory.

These are remedies for a weary soul and tranquil moments for a tired body. Who knows, if we stand still and listen—we may hear an angel's wings.

Today I send a voice for people in despair.

BLACK ELK
SIOUX HOLY MAN

April 4

Melancholy is a stray cat you once let in—now you have to fight to get it out. It is not impossible but very unpleasant.

Never look at that dark grieving attitude as a permanent fixture. See it as an outside force trying to control you. You would never let the cat take over your home—so don't let sadness monopolize your mind and spirit. Keep telling it to be gone. Say it again and again. Speaking the word is a powerful ally—and you've been doing it with dark words.

Fling all these things (destructive) away and live as your wise forefathers lived before you.

PONTIAC
OTTAWA
1763

April 5

Think for yourself. Stop living by tradition that promises you the moon and gives you a rock to carry.

Think things through—if one way looks easier than another, take the bolder way. Don't think what it is going to get you but what it is going to build in you. Some things feed the body and some the spirit. Go with the spirit—it already knows what you need to know.

Let us form one body, one heart, and defend to the last warrior our country, our homes, our liberty, and the graves of our fathers.

TECUMSEH
SHAWNEE
1808

April 6

Nature knows no other way than to restore what has been depleted. It simply works to put back what has been taken away. The moment man takes his eyes off the land, nature reclaims it.

Man has a way of waiting for help. Nature takes advantage of any opportunity to have its due season. And if any of us feel we have been held back, there is a due season. Take it. Don't wait for government to fund it or for a lender to say it is approved. Take whatever steps can be taken—physically and mentally, but definitely spiritually. Only here can you get foolproof help.

I hereby pledge my word, a word that has never been broken, that if your great father will set aside a part of my own great country, where I and my little band can live...we will live in peace with you forever.

COCHISE

April 7

Our methods of paying for life vary. Sometimes payment is emotional, and sometimes it is quite literal.

We fight for things not worth the effort and let the beautiful moments slip away without a word. The thought of failure haunts us and we groan because we cannot beat life into something that had no life from the beginning.

We are like the brown towhee that sees her reflection in the window pane and beats her wings against it time and again—because she is a competitor, not a realist.

If the Great and Good Spirit wished us to believe as the whites, he would have changed us.

BLACK HAWK
SAUK

April 8

Age magnifies who we have been all along. Our minds are planted with words that seed the very ground on which we stand. There should be regret for having planted seeds that will not allow change.

Responsibility to what we have planted is ours alone. It is a garden that we must weed—and it should not be a surprise to us that there are so many weeds and not many flowers. We have talked weeds and tangled our lives with brambles. But we have the same privilege of making sweeping changes—and we can.

Grandfather, Great Spirit, you are older than all need . . . you are older than all prayer . . . you are the life of things.

BLACK ELK
OGLALA SIOUX

April 9

Nothing stays impossible when hope emerges from a remote chance to a clear-cut burning desire that is so complete in detail the mind accepts it as real. Wishing and expecting are as different as the thorny vine and the fragile fern.

Don't let a living soul keep you from the mental picture that your dream is coming true. It can either be wishful thinking or it can be eager expectation. Expectation has every detail memorized and ready. Hoping and wishing is waiting and waiting and waiting.

An abiding love filled his being with the joy and mystery of living . . . and made a place for all things . . .

LUTHER STANDING BEAR
CHIEF OF THE TETON SIOUX

April 10

Don't give me your labels or those causes you travel under. I respond to you—not what you call yourself.

If you insist that I must accept your labels and all the wrappings that go with them, where is the room and opportunity to know the real person?

A rare friendship meets on common ground of hope and need and tender feelings—not on the strength of names and labels and challenges. We are simply friends. I see your smile.

To have a friend and to be true under any and all trials is the mark of a man.

OHIYESA
SANTEE SIOUX

April 11

One philosopher said that time is the wisest of all counselors, but that is not true. There is One greater and He cannot be changed to prove a point.

The same amount of time comes to all of us, and what we do with it can change the whole course of life. It can be the time when health is restored or a wealth of ideas is discovered. Or it may be the opportunity to tell someone we love them.

You must not hurt anybody or do harm to anyone. You must not fight. Do right always. It will give you satisfaction in life.

WOVOKA
PAIUTE

April 12

Time equalizes rivalry so that love and friendship finally have a chance to bloom. But the long wait is not necessary. It can happen as soon as one person is glad because another person is glad.

Love is not dependent on deserving it. If that were so, none of us would be loved and most would be barbarians. Who we are is not what someone else made us to be—but what we thought and said we could be. Love is cultivated so that we can communicate it to each other.

Everyone makes his feast as he thinks best, to please the Great Spirit, who has the care of all created beings.

BLACK HAWK
SAUK

April 13

Across the valley a thin ribbon of road rises to the rim of the horizon and disappears from sight. It looks like the edge of the world where everything stops simply because it is out of view. But other valleys, other hills, other roads exist beyond what can be seen from just one point.

What seems to be the end of the road is a bend in the road. Keep going and there is a broader view, a clearer vision. The outer eye can see only so far, but the inner eye has vision without limit. We can make our views good or bad, negative or positive. What do you see from here?

As for me, I assure you I will press on, and contrary winds may blow strong in my face, yet I will go forward and never turn back.

TEEDYUSCUNG
DELAWARE

April 14

What starts out to be an exaggeration, and even a great joke, can turn into a lie. The worst lie is to hurt someone intentionally, but equally sad is the lie told for pure self-defense, or to spare someone the truth. There are those who will believe a lie—which is more in their understanding than the truth.

So much drama and so much pretense makes lying acceptable to those living in false existence. To find the right path, get rid of the habit of lying. It is a trap that looks innocent but the effects lead to wrongdoing.

Our fathers gave us many laws . . . that it was a disgrace to tell a lie; that we should speak only the truth.

CHIEF JOSEPH
NEZ PERCE

April 15

Neither people nor animals take time to analyze right and wrong when they are cornered. They react in the only way they know how—most backing away when they have the chance.

On the other hand, some are not wise enough to see the chance to rethink the situation. They run roughshod and take what they want. Is there no tomorrow? Life balances things in ways we cannot understand. Use your heart—see that like attracts like—those who destroy will be destroyed.

Why should you take by force from us that which you can obtain by love?

KING WAHUNSONACOOK
POWHATAN

April 16

What limitations cannot be moved? Have we tried to move even a little the thing that dares us to do anything?

Someone will always try to say we are stuck with this thing so we may as well get used to it. But people adjust too easily to burdens when with a little divine wisdom they would know how to nudge it aside. Test your limitations—and keep testing them. Refuse the voices of solace that speak dolefully. Let nothing daunt your desire to keep trying.

We offer thanks . . . to the messengers of the Great Spirit who dwells in the skies above, who gives all things useful to men, who is the source and ruler of health and life.

IROQUOIS CONSTITUTION

April 17

Don't keep score. It is a tiresome thing, and if I give you something, it is yours, no strings attached. If you give me something I am grateful, but it is a kindness our friendship does not have to depend upon.

Who owes whom? Are we in competition? Is this a race where one person glows with accomplishment and the other sags from running and getting nowhere? No, there is no need to keep score. It wearies the soul and the spirit so that it cannot fit the slot of friendship.

O, the inexpressible comfort of feeling safe with a person, having neither to weigh thought nor measure words.

SHOSHONE

April 18

Appearances are deceiving and willfully suggestive. At the first sign of trouble, stand still. Don't jump to conclusions, because they are nearly always negative.

Create within yourself a place of harmony. You may not feel centered and poised, but speak the words anyway. Say to yourself, "Be Still. Steady." Peace can pass all understanding.

A troubled mind is little different from a strained muscle—it hurts. But stand still and let wisdom come in and do its perfect work.

If all would talk and then do as you have done, the sun of peace would shine forever.

SATANK
KIOWA

April 19

A long trail of experiences can tire us to the bone—but given the right attitude they can refine us as well. Our difficulties may not be cherished memories but they will create a deeper understanding to serve a purpose.

Nothing tests a person's mettle like standing firm when it would be easy to collapse. Nothing drains power like hindsight—but this is the important time to put things past in the past. Like the baby chick which pecks its way out of the shell to get its strength to stand, we feel the strain to know what we can do. The things that try us make us strong.

They approach like foxes, fight like lions, and disappear like birds.

EUROPEAN OBSERVER OF THE IROQUOIS WAY

April 20

A little brief authority can play such fantastic tricks before high heaven as to make the angels weep. The angels are not the only ones to weep.

Authority, among other things, is very brief. Clearly so when we try to control our thoughts and keep our tongues in check. Misused authority makes people self-destruct. It is not so much the authority we wield over others that destroys us, but our failure to wield authority over ourselves. What terrific power we have, but still we whine, "I just can't do it."

From Wakan Tanka, the Great Spirit, there came a great unifying force that flowed in and through all things . . .

CHIEF STANDING BEAR
TETON SIOUX

April 21

Evening hours in the country bring nature's songs. Coyotes, (probably three or four, but sounding like a whole chorus) stir up the neighborhood dogs.

The woods serve as a concert hall for amorous owls that call to one another in a variety of tones and squalls. And in the lull that always comes, the plaintive whippoorwill makes its plea. Its flight resembles staggering, but its song is the song of love. To the Indian, these sounds are all but symphonic and will be heard again in busier places.

Grandfather, Great Spirit, once more behold me on earth and lean to hear my feeble voice.

BLACK ELK
SIOUX

April 22

It is sweet when we come to the realization that we don't have to wait for someone to tell us we are worthy. We are children of the Spirit. So what if we made a mistake, lost a game, fell from grace.

Abraham Lincoln was defeated many times before he was elected president—proof that when a person sticks to his ideals they eventually happen. That particular part of the human spirit was made to overcome impossible barriers. It is a sleeping giant that can stand up and break all bonds. But we too often believe it is totally helpless.

Very seldom now do I catch one familiar note from these early warblers of the woods . . . they have all passed away.

SIMON POGAGON
POTAWATOMI CHIEF

April 23

Consistent effort grooves the stone. The tortoise and the hare proved that in the fable about who wins and who loses.

Another line or so could have been added to the story. The tortoise saw flowers and other slow travelers. He rested and ate in nice places. No one was there to rush him and he arrived at the appointed place in good shape.

Time passes and things change. How much better to enjoy it along the way instead of running in all directions and having nothing in the end.

Sometimes I look out over the Big Missouri and I see our Indian village . . . with smoke curling upward. . . . I hear the warriors yell and the laughter of little children. . . . It is but an old woman's dream.

WAHEENEE
HIDATSA

April 24

The strong green limbs of the young ash can put welts across the back if a person doesn't have a good bushpartner.

My privilege is to hold back the things that would hurt you. I would not want to look out for myself and never see to it that you came through the wilderness unscathed. If the journey brings no pain then the partnership has a bond. And if there is a bond there are fewer things to whip the soul.

Learn now, my brother, once and for all, because I must open my heart to you: There is no Indian who does not consider himself infinitely more happy and powerful than the French.

MICMAC CHIEF
1676

April 25

There is something about a mental picture, if you can get the right one, that can be so powerful that it changes a whole way of thinking. Part of a sentence or a few words spoken can be a catalyst for incredible change.

By chance I glanced in the Book of Wisdom, and it said to "throw off all encumbrances." What might seem impossible can be done—first in mind and spirit—then in the physical. "Throw off all encumbrances" means "We can do it." Those few words can make any of us an artist. We are given a beautiful mental image that we are definitely capable of bringing into being.

Each man is good in the sight of the Great Spirit. It is not necessary for eagles to be crows.

CHIEF SEATTLE
SUQUAMISH AND DUWAMISH

April 26

No Indian is too old to remember the little rabbit runs he followed as a child. They are there in memory as surely as he sees the sun and stars and moon today. Just the way the grass was bent and the droppings showed evidence of the rabbit made him keep going.

Few perfect things have ever existed—except in the mind of one who has lived the simplest and most profound journeys over a rabbit run. Perfection seems so important—yet it is in the memory that we have it. Living should be as good as we can make it—but real perfection will come when the sun is warm and time is sufficient to again walk that happy trail.

Even the little children who lived here and rejoiced here for a brief season love these somber solitudes, and at eventide greet shadowy returning spirits.

CHIEF SEATTLE
SUQUAMISH

April 27

It is the nature of circumstances to change and move and sometimes begin again. Like a whirlwind on open prairie, even sunlight changes its temperament and people strive to cover their faces and hope that when they open their eyes it will all have straightened out.

The changes are often left to us, but when we are on good terms with the Spirit we are given the blessing to know what to do. We are not born knowing these things, but like the food we take every day—so comes the wisdom. And like the food, we take it and digest it and pray over it. Such is the handling of circumstances.

May the Great Spirit shed light on your path.

BLACK HAWK
SAUK

April 28

Our faith is shaken and disappointment sets in when the pain we thought we were rid of comes back. Our bodies and souls have good memories where pain is concerned—and no matter how hopeful we were, our first response is to think we must have been mistaken.

We were not wrong, and we would never let a thief come back in to rob again. Fear is the thief and it steals. So we need to claim freedom from fear with the same intensity we claim other things that are rightfully ours.

My heart tells me I had just as well talk to the clouds and wind, but I want to say life is sweet, love is strong, man fights to save his life.

CAPTAIN JACK
MODOC
CIRCA 1873

April 29

Not even one person is isolated to the point that other worlds, other ideas, other persons, do not affect him. At one time the events of one small community was a whole world—but no more.

Pay attention to the inner personal world—and what is being built there by words and fears and questionable information. This is not new territory, but alien interference makes it seem like it is. Do not be persuaded by strange voices that promise everything and deliver nothing—no matter how good it sounds.

The sight of your cities pains the eyes of the red man. But perhaps it is because the red man is a savage and does not understand.

SEATTLE
DUWAMISH

April 30

There's no wisdom in judging too quickly. The overall picture may be an illusion and what we think we see is in our own minds.

Our judgment is poor when we get emotional and fall in love with someone, or call him bad before we know. Silence is a blessing until we are stable and have our perspective in balance. It is true that we have to judge sometime, but a little time can give us wisdom, which comes slowly.

The more I consider the condition of the white men, the more fixed becomes my opinion that they lose much by subjecting themselves to what they call laws and regulations.

TOMOCHICHI
CREEK CHIEF

FIVE
Hi' Ski

PLANTING MONTH
Ana sku'tee

*The Long Hair [Custer] came.
. . . They say we massacred
him, but he would have done
the same thing to us had we not
defended ourselves and fought to
the last. Our first impulse was
to escape with our squaws and
papooses, but we were so
hemmed in that we had to fight.*

CRAZY HORSE
SIOUX MILITARY GENIUS

May 1

Fear of obstacles makes us *u d nu lv hi*, lazy or indolent as the Cherokee calls it. Shy in nature and reticent in manner, most Indians avoid appearing forward. It is easier to put things off than it is to take the bit.

One of the greatest discoveries is to start out in faith. Start—and boldness and energy will come in. Start out—and wisdom will flow, spotty at first but it will come. If people who are afraid they are not capable will just start out to do a thing, it, or something even better, happens.

We are nothing compared to His power, and we feel and know it.

BLACK HAWK
SAUK

May 2

Gramps spoke lovingly of the "fellows" that swam up to the dock where his fishing lines were dropped over the side. He talked to them as though they understood every word—and they took the hook.

It is said of the fisherman that never catches anything that he never will. He keeps going but he keeps saying he is not lucky, and his spirit leads him to where there are no fish. He believes in chance, which all people believe when they don't know their own spirits. Not only does it work this way when he is fishing but in all he tries to do.

In order to honor Him I must honor His works in nature.

BRAVE BUFFALO
SIOUX

May 3

Respectful children learn from respectful adults. Calling rudeness only exuberant youth is setting the stage for worse things.

Respectful business once said the customer was always right. He was not always right; he could be exceedingly ignorant. But the practice of respect set the tone for business, just as respect can set the tone now. Men were gentlemen and women were ladies; a trait sorely needed now to head off the breakdown of self-respect and to restore kindness.

Love grows from roots of respect.

ANONYMOUS
CHEROKEE

May 4

The same law that attracts one person to another may operate when people are attracted to places. A certain place feels like home—and home has a drawing power that is exceptionally strong. This attraction is just as real and explicit as anything visible.

If we have ever been in this place of perfection once in a lifetime, it will live forever in the spirit. We run there when chaos threatens. Whether it is a place of peace or a hiding place—it is perfect harmony.

One does not sell the earth upon which the people walk.

CRAZY HORSE
SIOUX

May 5

Many weary and travel-worn Cherokees on the Trail of Tears ended their journey at a place called Blue Springs. Their first glimpse of these gushing springs must have made them question what could color the water the same hue as the blue bird.

So much of nature startles us with its unusual works. Boulders and bluffs and gigantic trees were a part of the Cherokee's past—but blue water the color of a blue bird? It may have been a natural phenomenon but to them it was a sign that the worst of the journey had ended. When something tells us to rest now, and to be at peace, it always remains a symbol, a promise that from now on things will improve.

When I make peace, it is a long and lasting one—there is no end to it.

SANTANT

May 6

The small things that make up our lives are pleasant and filled with sweet silences that soothe the soul. But even more commonplace, a lunch, a walk, the companionship of a sweet friend, our dog.

So many little things we take for granted and yet when we pay attention they all become new. The garden path, the sound of thunder, and the splat of rain on our hat brim. It is good medicine for a jaded attitude, good feeling to help us shed the chaos of the day.

The old Lakota was wise. He knew that man's heart away from nature becomes hard.

LUTHER STANDING BEAR
LAKOTA CHIEF
1898

May 7

Never forget the necessity of the blessing. Even though most of us have heard and used blessing all our lives, few of us know its significance. What is it really? And why is it so important when it has been used so lightly?

A blessing is a special grace given someone without their having earned it. It is the strength and power that kicks in when we set out to do a thing strictly on faith. We need it every day to fall on us abundantly so that we can overcome the darker nature.

It is through this mysterious power that we too have our being.

TATANKA YOTANKA
SIOUX WARRIOR

May 8

Always look behind the stick that stirs. You will not find the promoter, the wild card, the puff of wind, but you will find the mother who was the guiding light.

This mother is not a figurehead and not someone who exploits her children to be years older than their emotional makeup. She does not threaten nor does she have to consider it. Her children respect her standards and make them their own.

She is not always a beautiful woman—but a lovely one whose life is not a fad or a trendy excursion, but a journey that is memorable to many.

The ground on which we stand is sacred ground. It is the dust and blood of our ancestors.

PLENTY-COUPS
CROW CHIEF
1909

May 9

Daydreaming is the part of childhood we should never let go. Children have great dreams, and the strange part of it is they often turn out to be blueprints for the future. The imaginary playmates spur them to be more creative and to have more potential.

There is no reason we can't reactivate some of our dreams. Something about growing up tells us those dreams were not practical. Maybe they are now. What is to keep us from going back to that happy dream? If we say we cannot, we are being far too sophisticated.

Great Spirit...made the world to change...so birds and animals can move and always have green grass and ripe berries.

CHIEF FLYING HAWK
SIOUX

May 10

Our job is to be equal to opportunity—not the other way around. Good people have been put in positions that appeared ideal but it did not work. Unless a person has the spark of imagination and the ability to see and sense the precise working of something, there is little chance it will happen.

Standing on the rung of opportunity comes easily enough, but to keep our feet there is another story. It is the life and spirit in us that sets a wise pace and wants others to do as well. Our star has to shine by good use—not because we had equal opportunity.

The way, and the only way, to check and stop this evil, is for all the Redmen to unite in claiming a common and equal right to the land.

SHOOTING STAR
SHAWNEE WAR CHIEF
1812

May 11

Things can be so common, so constantly with us, that we forget to be grateful. Nature has one benefit after another, the trees removing toxins from the air, the earth filtering and re-filtering the water, and the beauty of flowers and lakes and wildlife delighting our souls.

Be grateful. It costs nothing and we cannot know how it keeps the door open for more beauty to come to us. American Indians were accused of worshipping nature, but it was the Source behind these things that never ceased to stir their spirits.

We return thanks to the sun, that he has looked upon the earth with beneficent eye.

SOSE-HA-WA
SENECA
1851

May 12

Calling someone a coward can be risky business. A coward isn't always a sneaky person; it may be someone who sees the end result of being foolish.

Circumstances today demand we be cowards to some degree. Why would we stick our heads in a noose when we know the outcome? Taking a chance may be a big thing to a fool—but why would anyone in their right mind insist on being a fool? Fools drink and drive, abuse children, and destroy lives and property because they can.

It is better to be called a coward than to be dead wrong—or dead.

If their minds are clean, and if they are obedient and promise to obey . . . they shall be welcome . . .

THE LAW OF GREAT PEACE
IROQUOIS
CIRCA 1570

May 13

*A*na *sku'tee*—the month of May, the beautiful month when much has been planted and will be planted. We pray for sunshine and showers of rain, for the opportunity to cultivate and start anew.

Ana sku'tee for the soul. May it be as beautiful as the season and as thrilling as the shimmering plums along the ridges that waft perfume and fluttering petals. Springs will spout water to the deeper places for an abundance of fish and the birds will sing in harmony. We truly are God's children; let us be grateful.

There was but one ruling power, and that was good.

STANDING BEAR
1933

May 14

Health fills the body and eager anticipation absorbs the person who sees the blue, blue sky and gives thanks. The sky is the flyway of the bird, whose freedom is to light and go at will, who swiftly builds a nest and lines it with soft down to cradle tiny eggs.

When evening shadows fall upon the earth and a lone jet cuts the puffy clouds with straight lines, it does not bother the birds. They chirp and murmur night sounds and settle down to sleep. Only the owl and the nightingale call in mysterious tones. And sometimes the mockingbird, having recorded too many songs, must relieve itself with a midnight medley.

We forget and think we are all there is.

JANE SEQUICHIE HIFLER

May 15

The earth is but a reflection of heaven, but the world is a reflection of unhappier places. The two are at odds and no one seems to know why—or even care.

The earth recoups when it experiences calamity. But the world slides away from reality with great pain and tears. It feeds its inhabitants with toxins and ugliness and tells them these are food and entertainment.

Wake up, children, wake up to reality. Rise out of the ashes and renew. It is your individual right.

The place to make a treaty is in the heart of their country, where we can dictate the terms; not they in our country.

Major F. N. Dodge

May 16

Time and time again we hear the same voices, see the same sights, hear the same sounds—and yet, we do not know.

Wisdom and knowledge, we seek you to know why things are the way they are and how to make them better. But we come to know that knowledge is a part of the past and wisdom is of the future. We do well to listen for wisdom—to never rebuke it however different it sounds. Our spirits are pure and simple and can follow in harmony. Help us to know the past but to follow wisdom—to sit quietly and hear its voice.

There is dignity about the social intercourse of old Indians which reminds me of a stroll through a winter forest.

FREDERICK REMINGTON

May 17

Morning peeks over the horizon with fresh breath and rosy cheeks. She sparkles with dew and turns the trees into halos of green that tint the air. Her eyes are blue and she turns them on earth with tender care. Her good humor reveals that it is the month of flowers—the planting month.

Speak to morning with gratitude. Though she comes daily, she stays only a few hours and then she changes clothes and moves across to the time of long shadows. Show reverence to the One who gave her to us, this time of day that gives us such vigor and such vision of how we can make the day!

So may our hearts and the hearts of the white men go out together to Thee and be made good and right.

BLACKFOOT
CROW CHIEF
1850

May 18

We quit too soon. When fear comes that we are cut off, limited, held back, we quit—and it is not time to quit.

A world of information flows to us every day and tells us where we are threatened, where we are apt to fail, what we cannot control. Are we going to believe that flow when it has been proven wrong so many times?

Each of us in our weakest moment has more power than we ever dreamed possible. All we have to do is to change our minds. When we change our minds, it changes everything. We don't have to accept dire predictions or listen to what "could" happen. We are power and we are wise—and we can use it.

My friends, your people have both intellect and heart; you use these to consider in what way you can do the best to live.

SPOTTED TAIL
SIOUX
1800s

May 19

Have mercy on other people when they do you wrong. No way must you hug them to you—but exercise patience and endurance.

Forgiveness is not reconciliation. But it frees you of responsibility and you move on without dragging something on your shoe. See it as experience you will never have to go through again. You have wisdom now and wisdom knows mercy. Wisdom knows your heart and knows the heart of others. If you bend low to forgive someone, you stand straight as an arrow and stay forever sharp and ready.

Our hearts sang in our breasts and we were glad.

KICKING BEAR
GHOST DANCER
1890

May 20

Most people want control. If they can control something, it seems to make things worthwhile. Important people have control, and though it appears no one is challenging their power the challenge is there in silent communication. A look, a laugh, an unspoken opinion hangs suspended until its time to express has come.

Real control is in the heart. It filters out the pretension, the sham, the show, the subterfuge. Intellect takes a back seat to honor which says a person can only control for the good of all. Control by sheer force is destined to break down—and the fall of it makes a great noise.

I feel grateful to the Great Spirit for strengthening my heart. . . .

PETALESHARO
PAWNEE
1800s

May 21

Spread a blanket on the grass and lie down to watch the sky change from one phase to another with light and color. Watch the subtle shading as the sun moves higher and higher. Watch the clouds scoot across in the invisible paths of the wind. Notice the heights the redtail hawk and the condor will reach and how they ride the currents with no apparent effort.

The sky in all its glory—sunsets and sunrises, moons, storm clouds, sunshine, rainfall and snow. They all come from a Source we do not see—but the evidence, the influence is clearly there. So why do we question our Source in all His provision?

The signs of the dawn are seen in the east and the breath of the new life is here.

TAHIRUSSAWICHI
PAWNEE

May 22

We were made to be different—you and I. The same diversity is in nature but it never argues about who is good, better, or best. Each one of earth's creatures goes about its own business—some yipping in the woods at night, some in high flight, some beneath water. One biological group does not look at another in abject disapproval—but all blend in a harmony that makes us peaceful to watch.

At times I may see you as bizarre and you may view me as lacking intellectually, but we are still God's creations, and it is the diversity that makes life colorful, and certainly not monotonous.

God made me an Indian . . . but not a reservation Indian.

SITTING BULL
HUNKPAPA TETON

May 23

Get up! Fight the belief that you are a lost cause. You have power you have not touched, and because of your toughened mind you refuse to change it. Stop fighting your own better nature. It is there, waiting for you to touch it, to use it, and to become whole.

No one made you poor or sick or lonely. You have simply let your lower nature walk in and take over and it has nothing but trouble in mind. Turn around and see that you are no different from most of the ones you dislike. Turn on your lights, walk away from trouble—see your new person. See the joy and peace and forget the past and let it slide away.

Why will you take by force what you may have quietly by love?

WAHUNSONACOCK
POWHATAN

May 24

To all appearances, deer have springs in their feet, the wind is made of smoke and mist, the flower-covered hillside is a handpieced quilt, and the sun throws shadows of hundred-foot trees. Illusion. Some of it is real, some is mystery—*u s qua ni go di.*

If it is illusion, it is still a part of the beauty of anything. Shadows and subtle movements, color and striking contrasts—these are given to us for enjoyment. It tells us to enjoy but to keep a clear head—know the gentle differences but use wisdom in making firm choices. We can see nothing good—or everything beautiful. It is our choice.

Wakan-tanka . . . teaches the birds to make nests, yet the nests of all birds are not alike. Wakan-tanka gives them merely the outline.

OKUTE
TETON SIOUX

May 25

I see you yet, my mother, walking briskly across the hayfield in the moonlight—with all the neighborhood children following like baby chicks. We were taken on these moonlight walks to teach us bravery and to help us see the hills and prairies in mysterious light.

She told us the bear always got the third one in line so we struggled to never be in third place. It kept us moving ahead, kept us laughing and ready to slide down a haystack or to wade a shallow branch with moss growing on wet rocks. Time has passed and so have you—except in spirit on a moonlit prairie.

I follow always, listening now and then with my ear against a tree.

BEDAGI
WABANAKIS NATION

May 26

Little children should be allowed to imagine, to let their minds run ahead to things that can be and things that never were. The imagination lets us see beyond the actual outline of things as they are. A mind freed of bias can detect times and times ahead.

Go back and recapture the imagination you never allowed to develop. Give it the freedom to examine your motives, your feelings, your heart. It will reveal joys and purposes and realign things gone wrong. There is no drab space in the imagination, no tears, and no losses—for that is the purpose of imagination, to remove and heal and let go.

The roots of a plant go down deep, and the deeper they go the more moisture they find.

SHOOTER
TETON SIOUX

May 27

Our hurts heal themselves in little ways—sounds, scents, a word at the right time. These things are like music that can reach deep inside where material things cannot go.

We too often let the cares of the world steal our peace and we lie down in frustration instead of taking charge. But healing waits. It waits for the right moment when our defenses are down and it fills our minds with hope. Start out in faith and the help will come. The beginning is by choice—and the only thing we give up is the idea that nothing can work for us.

You didn't understand our prayers. You didn't try to understand.

TATANGA MANI
STONEY

May 28

We tend to believe others are threats to our security—our personal *gu da lv to*. There has never been a time when so much threatens—but any Indian will tell you your security lies within you.

The Cherokee learns from animals in the wild. A sharp eye and a stealthy step cannot rouse wildlife when it has vanished into its own absence—in the spirit-sense. Perfect silence negates hostility and excitement—those things that stir danger in any area. We know this is true when we pass someone we know well and they never see us— we are not present to their senses.

I think we will still win. I think there are enough people who want to understand the Indian mind.

AN INDIAN GRANDFATHER

May 29

Life will not fail us if we do not fail it. It is like a fresh flow from a spring that starts so strong but puddles in those hard-to-cross places. We are open to catch debris and easily riled, but we can cleanse ourselves and move on.

We are life, and we can feed it or starve it. Regret starves—but peace and rest can restore. Look at sunlight and shadow playing across the plains, see the rose-colored patches that lie like swatches of fabric over the hills. Life is there, stir it up and give it a place. It is the way of the *Tsa la gi*.

Always changing; everything for good; nothing for nothing.

FLYING HAWK
SIOUX CHIEF

May 30

The past is ripe with wisdom and knowledge because it brings to the heart the reasons for many things we did not understand then. Search among the memories for the sharp stones that hurt so much you covered them as in a grave. Shame whispered to hide them—but wisdom would have said to use them for good.

One day you will say that it used to matter but it no longer rules. You can free yourself by taking old humiliations and using them like keys to open your own treasure boxes. And then you will love in a whole different and more wonderful way.

The red man must leave the land of his youth and find a new home.

SHABONEE
POTAWATOMI
1800s

May 31

Prepare yourself for what you need. If deep rest does not come naturally, give yourself reason to relax. Speak quietly and firmly to yourself of peace and release from stressful times. Comfort yourself with love the way you would comfort your child.

There is a power for peace, but it is not yours until you have recognized its Source. It is not an artificial substance, but a marvelous gift of a spiritual nature—and it is yours if you ask. Prepare yourself. It is the first step toward all good things.

The first American mingled with his pride a singular humility.

OHIYESA
DAKOTA

SIX
Su tali

GREEN CORN MONTH
Da tsa lu'nee

*I was born upon the prairie,
where the wind blew free, and
there was nothing to break the
light of the sun. I was born
where everything drew a free
breath. I want to die there,
and not within walls.*

TEN BEARS
COMANCHE

June 1

Long ago in Hopi country a young Indian boy went away to school and learned easily the way of the white man. But all tribes have a way of wanting to go back to beginnings when they are mature. Such was the case with Sun Chief and he related how his frame of mind shifted.

"I had learned many English words and could recite part of the Ten Commandments. I knew how to sleep in a bed, pray to Jesus, comb my hair, eat with a knife and fork, and use a toilet . . . and I also learned that a white person thinks with his head instead of his heart."

He never claimed that the power of articulate speech was proof of superiority over the dumb creation.

OHIYESA

June 2

We can change things around us in a number of ways, but it is change in ourselves that makes the biggest difference. To control the door to our minds and decide clearly and precisely what we let in and what can be put out is the beginning.

When we are tired of the same dumb mistakes, the same worn ideas, the need for change but nothing is done to start it, then the time has come to see if we really have a goal at all. The biggest obstacle is thinking we have gone too far to change. Clearly it is an idea that should be put outside the mind and the door closed firmly.

The path to glory is rough . . . may the Great Spirit shed light on yours.

BLACK HAWK

1833

June 3

The search for peace of mind has reached into areas grown dangerous. But like nearly all pursuits for peace, there is a hook on the end of many remedies. Too much sinks its claws in and will not let go—even to our destruction.

Most people do not want to hear there is a spiritual answer to their dilemmas. They prefer "other" ways that have side effects. The spiritual way is totally free of interference and very personal, as any Indian will tell you. *Ha dv da s da*—listen. Listen and hear.

Possibly you may be looking for someone with a strong heart. Possibly you may be intending to do something for me better than I know of.

BLACK KETTLE
PRINCIPAL CHIEF OF THE CHEYENNE

June 4

Break away from fear of someone's mouth. Let them talk, because it is to their own destruction.

Remember the saying, "Sticks and stones may break my bones but words will never hurt me." Bones will knit together again, but sometimes words are remembered for a lifetime. Criticism bends everyone—especially children—until a world of dreams is shattered and what could have been beautiful is ugly.

Close your ears to criticism. It only fouls up the fine tuning of the soul and spirit that makes living worth its salt.

I hold up my hand and I do not wish to fight.

LITTLE WOLF
CHEYENNE

June 5

Following a certain line of thought brings us to question theories and opinions that flow to us through open windows. What are we supposed to think or believe or follow?

We can get into trouble following someone who seems reliable and important and interested in us. A common bond may be the answer—but what do we have in common with someone so far removed from our own way of thinking? It is our personal responsibility to know where we are going—is it a path of peace or is it a place where nothing can grow?

Teach us the road to travel and we will not depart from it forever.

SATANK
KIOWA CHIEF
1871

June 6

Too little is being done because so many are looking for recognition and avoiding involvement where no one sees and applauds. Right this minute someone has a great need and has no idea how to get it met. Someone feels alone and without a person to tell them they can make it. A child needs reassurance and love and protection from real and imagined enemies.

Reach past personal woes and see these people and these situations and help—even without glory. The good of it will come back. It always does.

The evil spirit said, "I want half the people of the earth." The Great Spirit said, "No, I cannot give you any; I love them all too much."

KICKING BEAR
SIOUX

June 7

Fear makes us susceptible to the thing we fear. But the world of information is telling us we are potential victims of everything from killer bees to diseases we have yet to pinpoint.

Natural shields exist within us against anything on the attack. My mother proved it when I was a child and she was not afraid of snakes or dogs—but they were afraid of her. So was I, in a way. But I wanted that security so I had to learn how to use my natural shield against all threats, and her example was a worthy one. She put away fear by turning to face it and she gave it no power to ever make her susceptible to it.

It is my wish and the wishes of my people to live peaceably and quietly with you.

CORNPLANTER
SENECA CHIEF

June 8

If you need something and you have asked for it, then get ready to receive it. Getting ready to receive is a part of the asking, an act of faith that the answer is on its way.

It's no wonder that so few of our needs are met. We do so little toward preparing for it, and when it happens the first thing we say is, "I can't believe it!" Well, believe it, because it is assurance of receiving.

Sometimes dreams are wiser than waking.

BLACK ELK
OGLALA SIOUX

June 9

Timing is said to be the essence of excellence. But such wisdom has to do with whose timing it is. If we wait around until we feel the time is perfect, we may be waiting a long time.

Waiting can turn into lethargy and lethargy into sleep. What good is timing when a person is not awake. But when a beginning is made with honest effort—looking neither to the right or the left for approval or for signs that things are working, the grace will come. It will kick in at the precise moment it is needed to give substance and form to the faith.

Now is our time! Fight!

LOOKING GLASS
NEZ PERCE

June 10

Worry is a nagging reminder that something is not quite right. But as one elderly Indian said, "No use getting under umbrella 'til it rains." And when the clouds come, put your hand to a job that has been waiting too long and do it thoroughly.

Busy hands have eased many a worried mind and kept things in balance until something worked out. Even Emerson said that work is better than whiskey. There is a job well done—and no headache. What better way to be anxious for nothing!

He can stand torture, and is not afraid of death. He is no coward. Black Hawk is an Indian!

BLACK HAWK
SAUK

June 11

Deep wounds have been healed because someone cared enough to be patient and show kindness. How many times the pattern of our days has changed because someone comforted us instead of criticizing.

Gentleness is good to recall when someone close to us does something wrong. Why wound when we can heal? Love does not tell us we are stupid but that we made a mistake and we're standing together until it passes. Security comes from knowing love like this. And if the bonding is weak the first time—try it again.

Yonder sky . . . has wept tears of compassion upon my people for centuries untold. . . .

SEATTLE
SUQUAMISH

177

June 12

If a lack of humility has built a wall from which to scoff, remember that all walls come tumbling down. No safe place exists for those whose ease and comfortable standing place makes it seem safe to crow and scoff. As the old saying goes, "Every dog has his day." And, we can't afford even one to backfire when we need things to work right.

What we think is beneath us may be riding our shoulders in a very short time. Even the unloving person should see the signs and remember what seeds he has planted.

Complaint is just toward friends who have failed in their duty; accusation is against enemies guilty of injustice.

TECUMSEH
SHAWNEE

June 13

The need to touch and experience everything seems to tell us it is real. But what we see and touch is only the tip of the iceberg. There is more on the invisible than we have ever imagined—and a great deal more than we can comprehend when the truth begins to dawn on us.

This is why ideas are so important. Some buzz in and are gone before we can capture them—but others work in little by little. Some seem too fantastic to consider—and then, one particular one keeps returning. Don't shove it aside. If its intent is good, if it serves a good purpose, entertain it. Remember that sometimes we entertain angels unaware.

The Great Spirit directs me.

> YOUNG CHIEF
> CAYUSE

June 14

Like a pebble thrown into water, our thoughts ripple out, and when they have reached the far shore they ripple back bringing a little of whatever we sent out.

Caution is needed in sending out messages. Right responses depend on it, and if nothing is said at all we tend to fill in what we think they are saying. Nothing to prove it—and nothing to calm our fears.

Never leave a void; never leave someone in the dark about how you think. But do it gently—because what we send out ripples back to us.

Permit me to speak for a moment . . . weighing this question beside you.

PUSHMATAHA
CHOCTAW

June 15

Don't condemn yourself. Even if you have made a mistake—or a dozen mistakes, who has not?

We are too quick to profess stupidity. We are too quick to condemn our lack of will to eat the right foods, speak the right words, think the right thoughts.

It is true that we have to control these things, but why try to do it over burdens we put on ourselves. Begin to turn it around—praise each ability to do the right thing. Bring self-respect into play and call yourself free.

Think not that you can remain passive and indifferent to the common danger, and thus escape the common fate.

TECUMSEH
SHAWNEE

June 16

Strangers are often treated with more respect than our own families. And it is true that our brief meetings give us less reason to feel irritated than when, as the Cherokee expresses it, *ga ne lv*, we live very close to someone.

But those we love are still most important and must be tolerant of us—and often more so than we are of them. Patience and endurance are of the spirit—and tension and irritation of the mind. We cannot throw aside our wits and respond to total strangers with more concern than we do our loved ones.

Let your good judgment rule and ponder seriously before breaking bonds that have served you well.

PUSHMATAHA
CHOCTAW

June 17

Pressure destroys some people and helps others rally to do their best. One seeks peace and order and another heads toward noise and chaos. A little of both keeps us on our toes, but it means we have to have good judgment.

Peace is necessary—even under pressure. Like the rhythm of the sea, we rise to high tide and relax back to calm. No different from inhaling and exhaling, we are created to keep the balance.

I am much indebted to the Father of us all—Him who made us and placed us on this earth.

PETALESHARO
PAWNEE PRINCIPAL CHIEF

June 18

Survival is a decision. It seems not to be true when we are face to face with something or someone that is bent on destruction. But say to yourself many times a day, "No weapon formed against me shall prosper." It is a declaration of freedom and absolute intent.

When you are standing on the edge of a very steep mountain, get your balance. Walk firmly away from any situation that would push you over. You'll never know what a tremendous part your decision plays until you feel its power lifting you out of danger.

I am no child; I can think for myself. No man can think for me.

CHIEF JOSEPH
NEZ PERCE

June 19

To touch the earth is a lovely thing. The warmth of once again finding our beginnings, whether to walk or plow or plant. This place was created for us to have a place to stand and feel the pulse of the earth spread quietly through us.

Bitterness and fear are short-lived where we blend with the simplicity of natural things and know that we are supposed to take dominion—but never without knowing the mere privilege of walking down a country lane bright with sunflowers and field sparrows in song.

For all these favors we thank the Great Spirit and him only.

RED JACKET
1792

June 20

Most of us avoid major change. Our nature is to catch hands with something we are comfortable with and to walk a long way with it. Change can take place so naturally that it does nothing to upset the harmony, because we change with it.

But everyone has known change that shook their foundations and left them afraid and unhappy. This is the place where profound personal change can move mountains. The unproductive feelings and fears drop away and a new challenge enters to boost and enliven the one that knows he can do it.

The Red Man must leave the land of his youth and find a new home in the far west.

SHABBONA
POTAWATOMI
CIRCA 1800

June 21

Memories bind us—even when they are good. To step past certain memories brings up that emotion that says we are disloyal. It is not true, but we hear and take it to heart and go on hurting.

Time is supposed to take care of many things—but sometimes it doesn't. If it is something deep-seated and was traumatic from the very beginning, it is apt to ride us as long as it can. At times like these we have to make the decision to remove a memory by replacing it. Not by force—but by gentle but deliberate effort.

We, as the original inhabitants...and sovereigns of the sold...look upon ourselves as free as any other nation.

JOSEPH BRANT
MOHAWK
APRIL 21, 1794

June 22

Like the *tsi s qua*, the baby bird, we are sometimes held inside a firm shell with the job of pecking our way to freedom. Weak as gelatin and with no one to help, we begin freeing ourselves. One or two tries shows very little progress—except maybe we are a little stronger. And then with more pecking, we begin to gain strength and determination.

Is this not what we are supposed to do? Can we get strong with no effort? One or two more pecks and the shell cracks a little—but oh, it seems great. No one lifts us out and we are wobbly—but the mere act of standing up gives us something to sing about.

Do not ask us to give up the buffalo for sheep.

TEN BEARS
COMANCHE
1867

June 23

Our vitality does not go first—our interest goes. Dreams, one by one, that we let slip through our fingers, cannot be sustained and they drift. When that happens, what else is there?

Like rare pieces of old delicate lace, we fold away our dreams in tissue and forget them. Without realizing it, we have put away our vitality as well. Vitality—life, strength, creativity. Priceless interest must be restored if we are to be strong and healthy and able to contribute to our own benefit as well as others.

All living creatures and all plants are a benefit to something.

OKUTE
TETON SIOUX
1911

June 24

Tears are not always shed because of unhappiness. Emotions are stirred by the tears of other people and by music and gratitude and love. Hurt and humiliation and despair are washed away by tears—because that is the healthy nature of things.

We have been told there should be an end to our grieving, an end to the pain that brings tears, but time eases those things and cleanses at the same time. Long-term grieving is not natural and should not be the authority of what we think. But Spirit knows what we need—if we will ask.

My brother, you can go into the agency if you wish; but I intend to work my way up to the Powder River country. I think it will be better for us all if the people are not divided.

LITTLE WOLF
CHEYENNE

June 25

Every morning, liquid gold slips under the trees and pours down the slopes to puddle against the purple locusts. Shafts of sunlight caught in crystal dew light each blade of grass and splash color against the trunk of every tree.

The Sioux told their white invaders that they were digging in their Black Hills for gold to get rich—but the Sioux were rich by simply watching the Black Hills. And so it is with the morning sun. It brings a wealth that no material thing could give. Joy is gold and peace of mind cannot be evaluated. These things draw long-term interest.

I am grateful the Creator made me an Indian, because it is natural for a Cherokee to pray and believe in the supernatural.

CHARLES SEQUICHIE
GRANDFATHER

June 26

Make a quality decision to put aside anything that makes you worry the first thing in the morning. Keep morning as putty in your hands—that time to pray when your mind and spirit are rested. And if they are not rested, it is more important than ever to insist on morning freedom.

Lift your arms and give thanks that you are you and a new life is pouring into you this very moment. Bow down and be grateful for the freedom to do it. Keep fear out by rebuking it. Keep joy in by cultivating it. You are not helpless, you just forget to be blessed early in the morning.

Get a little further, lest I tread on thee . . .

QUOTED BY SPECKLED SNAKE
100-YEAR-OLD CREEK
1829

June 27

Discouragement knows exactly where our weaknesses are. Like a jackal it sniffs out the scent that fear creates and sets about a plan of destruction. It is a tool of the enemy and should be squashed at its very beginning.

When the spirit is like a deflated balloon, discouragement moves in swiftly. Be watchful and leave no opening, no sign of weakness. Take no offers to be underhanded—the pay is fraudulent, and defeat follows. Rise up and speak the word that you will not tolerate discouragement. Invite power and hope and eagerness—and see trouble dissolve..

A man ought to desire that which is genuine instead of that which is artificial.

SHOOTER
TETON SIOUX

June 28

To love is a privilege. To love kids and cats and dogs and chums, to adore an old one, to even love a material thing or place—this is life!

Love all you can. It is better than medicine, health to the body and soul, and it is scot-free. Laugh freely and with total enjoyment for this is a part of love. Forget the reasons why you should not love; though they are many, they give nothing and take everything. Sweeten your life—love something dearly and it will add to your well-being.

It is that kind of paradise which he only by his manner of life on this earth, is fitted to enjoy.

FLATMOUTH
PILLAGER
1851

June 29

Until a dog wags its tail, we are not sure it is friendly. Not so with humans. Many have learned that the friendly approach gets them everywhere. And among the many we meet are those with a mean spirit, regardless of the wagging tail.

Life is give and take—but in all honesty we need to tread lightly, especially if we are being offered a good deal for little money. Certain kinds know to ingratiate themselves before they begin to weave themselves into our lives. If this is holy the Spirit will tap you on the shoulder with assurance, but be aware that it may be unholy.

He pauses for an instant in the attitude of worship.

OHIYESA
SANTEE DAKOTA

June 30

Our full attention is like a powerful camera that focuses with such lighting and automatic adjustments as to be most potent for accomplishment. Inattention is sleeping on the job and the camera produces a fuzzy image.

Stop and think—what do you want? To do the job right? Or to hope you can outrun the competition? Yes, many are running, but only on personality. The right look, the right smile, the right lingo may work for a time—and then comes the substance. Make it real. Make it work. Give it your full attention.

I must give something of real value to show that my whole being goes with the lesser gifts.

CHASED-BY-BEARS
SANTEE YANKTONAO SIOUX
1867

SEVEN
Gul Kwa' Gi

CORN IN TASSEL
Tsa Lu Wa'nee

*It may be very small in your
ears . . . and we entreat you to
harken with attention; for we
are able to speak of things
which are to us very great.*

CORNPLANTER
SENECA NATION
1790

July 1

Because we can't see the possibility of something doesn't mean it doesn't exist. We just don't see it and what we do not see we cannot understand.

Grandmother used to say that someone "got the light" on something that had been muddled to them. They suddenly understood. Few of us suddenly understand because we are fighting the idea, trying to avoid believing something—only to have it become obvious.

And Grandmother, *El li si*, added, "and when you get the light, watch it, and if it dims—it's not the truth."

Our title to our lands is placed beyond dispute. Our relations with the Confederate States is that of a Ward; theirs to us that a Protectorate with powers restricted.

JOHN ROSS
CHEROKEE CHIEF
1861

July 2

And so it goes—the wrangling and arguing of the public and all its workings. We want to be informed, but when it moves from reality to grandstanding—we need a break.

Too many angry voices, too many accusations. We need rest for our ears, our minds, and our nerves. Every broadcast, every channel, every hour, it is repeated and repeated.

Take a walk and be comforted by the ordinary earth—which is not ordinary at all. It has healing powers that draw worn minds to birdsong and sunflowers, and a companionable dog that never listens to the news nor analyzes it for us.

Hear me, my chiefs, I am tired; my heart is sick and sad. From where the sun now stands I will fight no more forever.

CHIEF JOSEPH
NEZ PERCE

July 3

Innocence is ours in so many ways. Even the one that has no conscience, nothing good to measure life by—this person is innocent. Maybe not of wrongdoing but innocent of knowing God exists and knowing him intimately.

Can this be called innocence? Most would call it ignorance—and there's some mixed in. They know nothing of gentleness or kindness, but they recognize ruthlessness and the delight of being lawless. These innocent consider themselves sophisticated and beyond the ways of love. So very sad—because God is love.

Let us form one body, one heart, and defend to the last warrior our country, our homes, our liberty, and the graves of our fathers.

TECUMSEH
SHAWNEE

July 4

Our privilege has been to celebrate freedom for a very long time. But many see it only as a holiday—a time to stock up on drinks and food and a chance to be wild. Does anyone remember what happened and who gave life for this celebration?

We have a right to celebrate—but not without knowing why, not without recognizing what the original Americans gave up, what mothers and fathers and service people sacrificed. Every kind of sorrow paved the way for this day. Remember it and teach it and hold it forever before the world. We did not come to such wonderful freedom because we are so deserving. We celebrate because someone made it possible—and we should bless them.

I claim a right to live on my land, and accord you the privilege to live on yours.

CHIEF JOSEPH
NEZ PERCE

July 5

A world of things exist that we will never be able to explain. But all we have to do is look around us at world events, natural disasters, and at the cold, clear glint in the eye of ignorance, and know that to be somebody we need more than to become clever.

The big deals do not make us. Little steps, little thoughts, words and little acts—who we are and who we will become depends on the small bricks in our foundations. What do we have of contentment? It is the measuring stick for wandering souls who have lost the way and don't even know it.

I was living peacefully with my family, having plenty to eat, sleeping well, taking care of my people, and perfectly contented.

GERONIMO
APACHE

July 6

He was the storyteller relating tribal feats and conflicts with brave men and women overcoming every foe, climbing the highest mountains and swimming the swiftest streams. Some of the listeners were very young and aware of technological advances they were being taught in school. One asked respectfully but knowingly, "Grandfather, tell us about computers."

"I am a computer," the old man answered. "My body is a place of business where the work of circulation goes on all the time. The brain is in charge of all workings with more storage than a block-size building. It directs the entire business— but it is nothing if it is not connected to the Mainframe. If it has nothing but the worldly knowledge, it is no better than a mere human being. Connected to the Mainframe, it is unlimited."

I am but one man. I am the voice of my people. Whatever their hearts are, that I talk.

KINTPUASH
MODOC

July 7

Trumpet vines have grown so tall along the woodland path that a tall person must bend to walk beneath them. The path is not paved, not a place easy to walk. Step high over cushions of moss and protect the soles from huge acorns. Fallen sticks and uneven ground can hamper the stride—but, oh, it is beautiful.

There are dark shadows even on a sunny day. Shafts of sunlight shoot through holes in the canopy and the tangle of grapevines and woodbine dominate space. Here, the spirit is freed to be whatever age, whatever time, whatever purpose chosen for the moment. It is a time machine, a heavenly carriage, a very private sanctuary. It is a mind and spirit set free from compression and depression—a safehouse from the world.

My friends, if you took me away from this land it would be very hard for me.

STANDING BEAR
PONCA

July 8

When Pharaoh was asked when he wanted the plague of frogs removed from his land, he said, "Tomorrow." Why not this minute?

Why put off, delay, procrastinate, when the problem can be resolved this very minute? We can be smarter than Pharaoh if we choose things to be changed now. Now is the opportune time to speak the word, to work the word, to change destinations.

If not now, when? Because tomorrow, there will be another tomorrow—or someday. Borrowing from time delays living—but now changes the face of many things.

Why don't you talk, and go straight, and let all be well?

BLACK KETTLE
CHEYENNE

July 9

Dream dreams and see visions. Not the black ones—but images of plenty, pictures of being totally well, fully secure.

Dream that the horse chestnut tree is in full bloom, that the stone basin is overflowing with pure water, that the flood at its high point is carrying off the debris of life.

If a dream is frightening and wrong, go over it bit by bit and change it. Get rid of the damaging catalysts and reach higher. Build good dreams. Lift out the cobwebs—don't smash them. Life is putty in your hand—shape it.

I am an Indian and looked upon by the whites as a foolish man—but it must be because I followed their advice.

SHUNKA WITKO
SIOUX

July 10

Good people sometimes tend to believe the goodness is by their own power. Bad people know they stand on thin ice and secretly wish for help. Stupid people throw themselves into riotous panic with complete abandonment to evil.

Where is the gentleness and compassion and sweetness that is needed right now? It is in the hearts of those who know they cannot make it without spiritual strength, without keeping the laws, without knowing where the real Power exists. It is crucial to know which group appeals to us—and to make some decisions now.

It was you who sent out the first soldier, and we who sent out the second.

TEN BEARS
COMANCHE

July 11

Like a tongue on a sore tooth, night magnifies. The light of day dissolves worry, but night enlarges fear. Loneliness is greater at night and stress swells like yeast in bread.

Warm, reassuring, comforting light can be present night or day. As dense shade in deep woods can cause the owl to call out its nighttime song, so the dark makes us feel vulnerable. But one bright beam of sunlight can pierce the forest and hush the owl—so one bright beam in our spirits can dissolve darkness. We are not alone—and nothing is impossible.

The earth and myself are of one mind.

TOOYALAKET
NEZ PERCE CHIEF

July 12

When forced to wait, do it with patience. But do not waste the time. This time is for a purpose, a time to remember words of truth and grace, a time to let the fount of faith refill the arid spirit.

Patience comes willingly when a minute is used wisely. It forces nothing but lets power, drop by drop, refill a weak body and depleted soul. Practice receiving, practice gratitude, say what you want—not what you think you are going to get or what you deserve.

Wait patiently—but never empty of purpose.

You had many buffalo to eat and tall grass for your ponies—you could come and go like the wind.

WOVOKA
SON OF PAIUTE MESSIAH
1889 (TO GHOST DANCERS)

July 13

Everything needs attention. We need attention, we need a touch of the divine, a reassurance that we are children tenderly revered. Our needs are met and our love and compassion are turned outward to care about things and people around us.

Giving attention is a sacred promise, a word spoken to us, for us, and by us. The word creates and brings out of the invisible everything that operates a world of activity. Nothing can stop it but our denial. This makes saying something very important—important that we speak right. Not only to cause right conditions but to remain children tenderly cherished. Words are life and death—choose life.

It makes my heart sick when I remember all the good words and broken promises.

CHIEF JOSEPH
NEZ PERCES
1885

July 14

Eating the greens Grandmother gathered was a trial, an imposition on a child remembering the fried or roasted meats of wintertime. But she persisted in gathering them and she insisted that I eat them because their medicinal properties would ward off many diseases.

Grandmother would have been appalled at many things from fast-food to the tasteless cooking of greens. She was the matriarch and in many ways remains so, because her mindset set our minds and even now an unwanted salad comes with the command, "Eat!" We remember and are the better for it.

Our village was healthy and there was no place in the country possessing such advantages.

MA-KA-TAI-ME-SHE-KIA-KIAK
SAUK AND FOX CHIEF

July 15

Personal choices have shaped our lives. Some were made too fast, without time to see the good and the bad. Certain things were dressed in bright colors and drew us like bees to nectar. We chose, we sighed, we cried. It was mere color and taste—not substance.

Time teaches wisdom—or does it? Youth or age or circumstance plays little part. It is the lust that twists judgment and sets us up like clay ducks. This thing, that person, this situation—would make all things perfect? It is a personal choice, a path chosen and not easy to walk—sometimes impossible.

The white man build big house, cost much money, like big cage, shut out sun, can never move, always sick.

FLYING HAWK
SIOUX CHIEF

July 16

In ages past predictions were made that a time would come like the days of Noah—a time of floods and volcanoes and earthquakes. Evidence of hot spots, upheavals and changes in the earth is everywhere—and it makes us ask if this is the time like Noah's.

Earth goes on renewing and making every effort to stay whole and clean in spite of the tampering of mankind. But the world is another cup of tea. Can it change itself? It must learn from earth that too much pressure can blow everything. We learn from the river that we can be so broadminded that we spread into the shallows and dry up in the midday sun.

Our decision is to read the signs and know for ourselves. It comes down to a very fine point—a point that is us.

Behold, my brothers . . . the earth has received the embraces of the sun and we shall soon see the results of that love!

SITTING BULL
SIOUX

July 17

Love has no part of abuse. Claims of great love are really claims of great need when there is abuse. Love doesn't abuse. It protects and comforts and gives support. Abuse is from possession of evil—the need to hurt and destroy. It is a need for a prey—a smaller prey where domination is secure.

Human need is a net thrown over a thing or a person to keep them close and subdued. If escape seems possible the possessor turns to tears and persuasion as another way of dominating. But love—love is a deep sacred trust that runs through the most common acts, the shared hours, the sweetest and most trusting touch. It is the miracle of life.

Why does the agent seek to take away our religion?

SITTING BULL
1889

July 18

A certain careful handling of business takes over when something makes us feel limited. Whether it is time or money or people, we know they must be utilized in the right spirit. As the Indian says, "Everything is in a circle." Whatever we set in motion comes back, and often shocks us by how quick and with what impact.

Such things teach us to stop and think—to consider the use of a word or an act—and even a dollar. When we have material needs, a single dollar given where the need is great can multiply and come back to us a hundredfold. Even treating someone kindly is an investment, and though it may seem insignificant, when we are weary and sore, we learn how important it is.

You have noticed that everything an Indian does is in a circle.

BLACK ELK
OGLALA SIOUX

July 19

Talk is easy, but listening is better. Mouths have a way of getting away from us—and then we say things we are not committed to—or don't necessarily believe.

Others may seem sensitive—too sensitive. But we may be dull and careless. When the mouth starts to work, the mind stops to listen. Where did those words come from? They came from trouble on the horizon. True, some are easily offended—and on the other hand, what would it have cost to be quiet?

I am the maker of my own fortune.

SHOOTING STAR
SHAWNEE WAR CHIEF

July 20

Having done all, stand. Stop saying you wish you had done differently, stop the anger, and above all, stop acting like a donkey. Having done all, stand still and see it work, support it by keeping faith on your lips—not pitiful insecure words.

When a thing is right, it is right. Stand on it and make it a part of your innermost spirit. How can your consciousness work to any advantage if you keep running in circles and doubting what you had to do? All the circumstances will come into play and make final decisions, but standing for right was your part—and you did it!

For all these things we thank the Great Ruler and Him only!

SA-GO-YE-WAT-HA
SENECA CHIEF

July 21

She was *e li si*, a woman elder, a leader with great gifts, and what she spoke rang with truth. She said, "Every person makes a strong statement about who they are." The words were simple and unpretentious but they were powerful, for every day we hear people telling us who they are. Some say, "I am sick"; others say, "I am broke." Some have said over and over, "I am afraid."

Their claims are as good as done. They can make new claims of health and plenty and strength, but they seldom do it. But when these very personal statements come to our ears, we can remember to write out our personal beliefs of well-being and never part with them for a minute.

You must speak straight so that your words may go as sunlight to our hearts.

COCHISE
APACHE

July 22

Years ago, a very wealthy man was asked about the condition of his soul. He responded as he always had—with the idea that money can buy anything. A large sum of money was offered if anyone could give him tangible proof that he even had a soul. His business acumen was not in keeping with the spiritual, so he did not know his soul was a combination of mind, will, and emotions—the very things he used to accumulate his wealth!

Many real things are not tangible—fragrance, the wind, sounds; but we feel their influence and know them to be actual and sometimes more enjoyable than that which is touchable. To hear the wind chimes, to smell the bed of petunias and honeysuckle, to feel the breezes—these lovely things prove that we do have souls.

My friends, your people have both intellect and heart; you use these to consider in what way you can do the best to live.

SPOTTED TAIL
SIOUX

July 23

Anxiety is as contagious as measles. Even when we are calm and secure, listening to what could happen—what likely will happen—can drag us into deep anxiety.

Be on guard against the spread of rumors and what "could" happen. Sure, things can happen and most likely will if we start listening to the sensational reports that the whole population could be wiped out by overeating. We could also be bruised by running into the bones of skinny people—but neither is apt to happen.

Use some common sense, refuse to be roped into thinking every report is gospel. And give yourself credit for using your head in hearing anxious reports.

We preferred our own way of living.

CRAZY HORSE
SIOUX

July 24

Even in July there are lovely cool places in the woods. May apples spread their leaves to shade the tiny blooms of sweet william, and moss, rich and green and cushiony, gathers in rocky areas.

Most wet-weather springs have drawn back into the earth and an occasional tiny trickle waters the wild plum and invites the goldfinch to bathe. It is a haven on a very warm day for both red and gray squirrels to romp and play—but not with each other as they are natural enemies.

Get away from the rise in temperatures and let mother nature soothe your brow with songs of the meadowlark and the field sparrow. It is good medicine—very good medicine.

What I say, I want you to take to heart.

CHIEF BLACKFOOT
MOUNTAIN CROW

July 25

Victor Hugo said that certain thoughts are like prayers, and at times, regardless of the attitude of the body, the soul is on its knees.

This happens frequently when we need courage. And courage, like muscle, works best when a demand is made on it. Unless we demand, we may never know what we can do. That demand may be so effective that we never go back to a time without courage. And out of gratitude, our soul will still be on its knees.

I took to the warpath as a warrior not as a chief. I had not been been wronged but some of my people had been…and I fought with my tribe.

GERONIMO
APACHE

July 26

Over the years we forget how many times we follow the same paths. So accustomed to the twists and turns most of us could walk with our eyes closed—except for the gnarled plum that grows too close to the path.

Somewhere in our deepest memory are all the little paths, the little rabbit runs we have walked. Plans were made, fears were put aside, tears were shed, and decisions made along these paths. When we were children, around the bend was a long way from home. Even now we sense we have strayed too far. But we are still within earshot of those paths that lead us back to everything that waits with open arms.

Before our red brothers pass to the happy hunting ground, let us wash off our war paint in the river. Let us break our arrows.

PLENTY COUPS
CROW CHIEF

July 27

The human race needs a loving hand. Not a permissive hand and not a hand that strikes out. But it needs a hand that soothes and leads and does so without a selfish motive.

Our condition is a result of disobedience. Every rule has been broken, every law, written and unwritten, has been ignored. It has all made for imbalances, injustices, broken hearts and less stability.

Where is the loving hand? It is our own. It begins with the individual who is willing to let others exist, to forgive and to be forgiven. No doubt the bad will get worse, the good will get better—and all in all it is a personal decision.

By peace our condition has been improved in the pursuit of civilized life.

JOHN ROSS
CHEROKEE CHIEF

July 28

Some of us see solitude as a primary need—a time away from noisy routine to get our priorities in order. We want our quiet moments, but we want them by choice—not forced on us by circumstance.

We get to know ourselves in solitude. We question what brought us to this place, because we know it was not by accident. When we are with others we contemplate their way, but alone, we follow our own way. In quietness our strengths are fortified and made ready for those times when the sands run fast.

I am the man that makes it rain . . . I cause it to rain so the corn will grow.

LONE WOLF
KIOWA

July 29

It helps to turn away from daily events to the quiet of nature and feel the peace that permeates the wooded land, the silent hills, and all the wildlife that lives there.

At midday, a woodchuck suns himself. A coyote walks the craggy hill with tail tucked under as though he is already proven guilty. A raccoon sits on a high branch watching the world of nature. And it may be a place of quiet—but never of inactivity and never without reason. But somehow simply watching it balances human problems with inner spirit, and it is something to recall when disorder tries to rule.

I want to tell you all that is in my heart—and if I do not, it is because I hide it.

LITTLE RAVEN
ARAPAHO
1867

July 30

The sights and sounds and fragrances of the countryside are extraordinary after a summer rain. Wildflowers and morning glories profusely spread along the fencerows—and the bittersweet has orange berries popping out of little hulls.

It is a tranquil time, a time to catch the scent of petunias heavy on the evening air. It is something that will be repeated over and over for as long as we can remember.

Early morning brings the sweet call of quail and the cries of a killdeer doing wheelies over the meadows. Speak these things and remember them, because it centers the soul like nothing else on earth.

The bird in its flight stops in one place to make its nest, and in another to rest in its flight.

DAKOTA WISEMAN
1890

July 31

To be truly beautiful, a precious stone must be cut precisely, polished expertly, and set in the right mounting. It was no less worthy in its original state, but its hidden beauty was where we could not see it.

People are precious stones as well. They may be covered by a rough exterior, but we sense the glow—even before they are polished and shaped.

With so much emphasis on how we look, there is always work to do, and it isn't all on the outside. Pettiness is the ugly bubble in an otherwise lovely diamond. Bitterness hides sparkle—but careful handling brings out the beautiful facets—and love makes it a treasure.

We saw the Great Spirit's work in almost everything: sun, moon, trees, wind, and mountains.

WALKING BUFFALO
TATANGA MANI
STONEY

EIGHT

Su'nali
END OF FRUIT
Galo'nee

*From tempers be it known that
we are warm in the field of
battle and cool in the hours of
debate.*

PUSHMATAHA
CHOCTAW CHIEF

August 1

No wonder fear throws a wrench in our well-laid plans. We have been relying on dead gods, on lifeless theories and trying to fit our keys into corroded locks.

This isn't living, it is throwing in with empty promises with nothing to back them up. Here we are, spiritual creations, trying to survive on mental and physical remedies, never considering that we have access to treasuries of ideas and wisdom and spiritual knowledge. These are the appointment makers that say, "go here, go there," and we can go in confidence.

Spirit, come out of your web of supposed protection and begin to use the gifts. They are yours and they are beautiful beyond the reasoning human mind.

I am you!
I am yourself!
Don't let me waste
Upon the shelf.

NELLIE SEQUICHIE
CHEROKEE

August 2

Knowledge is evidence of the past—but wisdom is using it to see the future.

Knowing what to put in your bouquet of life takes wisdom. Drugs and alcohol and unrestrained behavior are the poison ivy among a field of life-giving herbs and beautiful flowers. These things are known to be toxic and death—but someone who had worldly knowledge knew they made a person have hallucinations. This need to look into hell is like calling home for comfort—it's not going to happen.

Say it: "I am a person with the power to draw on unlimited wisdom—and I do it now by turning away from the dancing images of total foolishness and destruction."

If the child cries for mercy, that child must have mercy.

HANDSOME LAKE
SENECA
1800

August 3

She is one of those persons whose entire time is given to informing the world about what she does not like. It is not a simple opinion but an oration spread over a long time and over many acquaintances.

Because people are often tolerant, she sits in a gathering with confidence—confidence that assures her how many need to hear, "I don't like… "

O persons, your words are frozen in time, a halo of light or darkness that swirls through the ethers like immense flocks of tiny birds hunting food. But those words come home to roost. They do not sing, but they squawk in complaining sounds and echo in the heads of those who cannot like the simplest thing.

My children, as you travel along life's road never do harm or cause anyone sadness.

ANONYMOUS
WINNEBAGO

August 4

When the going gets rough, bear down. Every woman that has ever given birth knows you don't stop because it hurts. You give it all you have and when the breakthrough happens— what a wonderful prize!

The swimmer knows he cannot stop or he will sink. And if he has to pause, he rolls over and floats until new strength comes to go on.

Work awhile, endure awhile, believe always, and never turn back. The best is yet to come. You wouldn't want to quit and then find out later you only had inches to go.

It is the wind that comes out of our mouths now that gives us life.

> ANONYMOUS
> NAVAJO
> 1897

August 5

Those who revel in working the world of the internet and e-mail have believed they deleted certain things they sent out—but the words were deleted only on the surface. These things can be retrieved and often are.

Indians have always known this to be true—that if you send out any kind of word, it is frozen there in the ethers, forever preserved. Silence is truly golden—though most of us discovered it after too many things had been spoken. But if our remorse is genuine and we ask to be forgiven, those words can become useless and irretrievable. It is important that we remove the power of past words and replace them with thanksgiving.

The first peace . . . is that which comes within the souls of men when they realize their relationship, their oneness, with the universe and all its Powers.

BLACK ELK
LAKOTA

August 6

When you are a child of the land you come to appreciate the moments of pleasure when the early morning sun gilds the tree trunks and throws shadows across the garden. And when evening comes with its cool shadows and nocturnal sounds you revel in your native ways.

The woods at night ring with golden bells all blending in a joyous sound that is the locust chorus. And suddenly it all stops and for a brief moment there is total silence and then the high plaintive mewl of an owl. It is an evening concert and you are alone with it—except for those who lived on these wooded ridges and loved it too. The conductor is the hour that leads it all in a song of the heart.

There is no other place for us.

BLACKTOOTH
1900

August 7

Coming home is near to being a gift of the spirit. Hours have passed and duty has been performed. It is the hour of return—the hour when the circle is completed and coming home is the hour of grace.

Sometimes the circle is just a little one—a time of going out and coming back. It doesn't take long. But years can lie between the going out and the coming back. It is the innate compulsion in an Indian to return to his beginnings—the essential completion of going back. Indeed, of coming home. And he can hear the voices, catch the fragrances, and feel the presence of his forebears and it is a thing of grace that renews and restores his spirit.

When I look upon you I know you are all big chiefs.

SANTANTA
KIOWA

August 8

Life is complicated, no doubt about it. We start something and it leads us into something else—and that into another thing, and we ask, "How did this happen?"

On the other hand, we wouldn't like it any better if we were confined to a treadmill that goes and goes but gets nowhere. It is life lived at a time when order as we once knew it, is nonexistent.

It helps to go back to where we started and take each bend and turn and change things—even if we have to admit we were wrong and ask someone to forgive us. All is not lost, and it helps to admit we made moves that were wrong. And even against our most selfish nature—begin to make them right.

Do not wrong or hate your neighbor; for it is not he that you wrong: You wrong yourself.

SHAWNEE CHANT

240

August 9

Conversation does not reflect the grand training our mothers and grammar teachers hoped we would remember. But we are aware that when we say "ain't," it ain't right. Frequently, those little words express what we want to say better than what is considered correct.

Why is it that we notice these things when dozens of vulgar and offensive words are used without anyone showing surprise. Maybe people are not aware that words are creative and shape who we are—coarse and without polish or gentle and caring. We have a responsibility to keep ourselves clean and it begins with our words.

The mental capacity of the Indian is of superior order.

COL. RICHARD DODGE
1882

August 10

Voices echo in our minds even after we are grown. They can be whispers that only the subconscious mind can hear—but it is an exacting voice that can give us courage or suggest failure.

We've no idea how fenced in we are by those voices of old. The subconscious mind is a road map, a map with many mistakes, and who is to know what they are? Nothing is set forever in one direction, and we are able to read the signs and change them. Not because they may sound old-fashioned but because they are foolish and suggest that we take paths that have no destination except ruin. We can change it and we must.

If the Indians had tried to make the whites live like them, the whites would have resisted, and it was the same way with the Indians.

WAMDITANKA
SANTEE SIOUX

August 11

Two people in agreement sets a trend. It works well, and it works for the good or the bad. Be very careful how you agree with someone, particularly if it is destructive.

We put down dozens of claims every day, though it may sound like speculation. The markers are there by our own mouths and though it seems like only words, it sets a trend. If we could go back and see what we talked about, what we were afraid of, what we said was possible, we could see where we put down the roots as well. We have been told that where two agree as touching anything on earth, it is established. Do we want that?

As far as I am concerned, if they are hungry let them eat grass or their own dung.

ANDREW MYRICK
TRADER

August 12

In this age of free-thinkers, many a business and political genius has asked, "Who can I join hands with that will do me the most good?"

Almost any aggressive person can get his feet on the ladder of success. It is keeping them there that gets into artfulness. Because there is a time to think and act independently, a person's footing may get very shaky and very temporary.

A law of cause and effect works minute by minute, and that simply says we get only when we give and we reap only what we sow. No one else can do for us what we have to do for ourselves. And no one else can keep us sharp and honest and respectful. It is our job.

Once I moved about like the wind. Now I surrender to you and that is all.

GERONIMO
APACHE

August 13

Grief is one of the most tenacious and persistent emotions of all our feelings. Putting it aside is a temporary act at most, because it waits and moves at subtle times and when we least expect it.

This deceptive pain can spring from times and times ago—things that have been dealt with and put to rest. But grief is a spirit and loves to spring up as guilt and subtle questioning about what if we had done differently.

We have a right to happiness, without grief. The fact that we can scold it and have it leave should show us we can be free, even though it takes a time or two to overturn its invitation to hurt.

Almighty God made me an Indian, but not an agency Indian.

GERONIMO
APACHE
CIRCA 1876

August 14

The direction of our lives is more dependent on our own thoughts and words than on what the government does and how it affects the economy. Yes, we do live in the system, but that doesn't mean we have to get down and struggle for every dollar nor fret about who will take care of us.

There's no less money in the world than there has ever been, but by design we have developed a very negative view that if everybody else is having a struggle, then we must struggle too. It is buying into the same club that says age means sickness. No, it doesn't. Many older people are not sick at all, because they never planned to be.

What are our plans? It pays to know.

Indians living close to nature and nature's ruler are not living in darkness.

WALKING BUFFALO
STONEY

August 15

Evening brings Sam-cat to the kitchen door loudly demanding attention. Not that he wants to be fed, because most of the time he prefers the food he finds for himself. He comes to be spoken to, to be petted, and to be made welcome. He's no different from you and me.

To be welcome is a basic need. If someone wants us simply for our presence we have something golden. Even when we are hungry we can stop to be greeted because it is a sign we are worthy of attention. Even the aloof and arrogant melt when they know they are loved and wanted. Sam proves that every time he leaves his hideaway in the barn or woods and comes home to renew his security.

Kinship with all creatures of the earth, sky and water was a real and active principle.

CHIEF LUTHER STANDING BEAR
LAKOTA

August 16

The most common reason for not liking someone is because we don't know them. We may tell ourselves we don't care for the way they look or we don't want to know them because they think they are special. These are just excuses.

It's a tragedy to judge people by the way they look. Underneath every mask is a real person with real problems and real needs. We may look secure and it makes them uncomfortable. If they only knew, we have the same fears, the same thoughts that they do.

Every friendship could take shape more quickly if we would speak and smile—even when there's no obvious response.

The Great Spirit, in placing men on the earth, desired them to take good care of the ground and to do each other no harm.

YOUNG CHIEF
CAYUSE

August 17

If you have been handed a difficult situation, stand firm. Change can shake you, but it can't tear you down. Common sense will come in to create a safety zone—a haven for a time to adjust.

This is decision time. Speak gently to yourself and never say you should have known. Don't lie down and quit and don't go to pieces. You have spiritual strength whether you know it or not—rely on it.

This is a time to declare your strength to use your head, your heart, and your spirit. It is your right and privilege—so let no one talk you out of it.

The great sea has sent me adrift; it moves me as the weed in a great river.

UVAVNUK
ESKIMO

August 18

Flowers keep us close to the earth and show us what repetition can do. When we are good planters and caretakers we see results—not just once but many times in many ways.

We see the garden in our minds before we plant, and we see its needs and what we can do to make it better. But the garden in the mind stretches farther then just flowers and vegetables. It needs the same careful cultivation—never letting the weed of illness or strife or discord take root. This garden blooms year round and we should refuse to let it become a weed patch.

It is a day of beauty and bright sunshine. I rejoice that we can all meet here as friends, eat our bread and meat in communion, smoke the council pipe and the pipe of peace.

PLENTY COUPS
CROW NATION chief

August 19

It is so easy to forget that every thought and word has a lasting effect. The result may not be noticed immediately, but time has a way of playing back the tape when we least need to hear it.

Nervous tension and anger, however unintentional, may seem justified, but it never is. Too much stretch on a rubber band can bear on its weakest place and snap back to sting. Avoid putting too much pressure where it is dangerous. It is destructive and it hurts too much to take the chance.

When the tape starts saying, "They meant it for harm," respond, "But I mean it for good."

This is a glad day for me...because there is no more war between us and we meet in peace.

CHIEF TWO MOONS
CHEYENNE

August 20

Talking trouble is rehearsing trouble. Innocent as it sounds, it draws an outline for the thing to happen.

Medical information in the wrong hands lays out a mere possibility but is always a catalyst for hope and false hope at that. Remember that most of what we hear is simply read to us as a bed-time story meant to help us rest—but it never does.

Someone said talk is cheap, but it isn't. It is one of the most expensive items we can handle. And talking trouble may be entertaining but it is costly—and never worth what we seem willing to pay.

I am master of my condition, I am master of my own body.

ADARIO
HURON CHIEF
1600s

August 21

A person has to have enough confidence in himself to go ahead and run a good race, even when he knows it is going to be grueling and that he might not be the winner. But that is so much better than sitting down and saying to himself that he isn't good enough to try.

Most people tend to lean on the belief that they are not good enough. But no one starts out good enough. It is the getting up and getting into living that makes us good enough. At times self-esteem melts like ice in the sun, but it certainly does not mean we do not qualify. The fight is not with others—but with ourselves. We have to overcome ourselves and all our hidden voices that tell us we are not going to make it.

I am here on my own ground and I will never go back. You can kill me here but you cannot make me go back.

DULL KNIFE
CHEYENNE

August 22

In a sense, the American Indians lived a freer life than any other race. They had no boundaries, and many lived in teepees that were cool in summer and warm in winter. They moved south in cold weather and north when it was hot. They ate off the land and kept it in good condition without becoming slaves to it. They wore the very best furs and rode the best horses, and they worshipped God in the purest sense.

Every morning the Cherokee prayed near the stream and then bathed in it—summer and winter. He protected his honor and that of his tribe. He did not litter the land nor contaminate the streams, and he fought when he had reason to fight. Because he lived so close to nature, he was something of the poet and loved deeply.

These were Indians and they left us that legacy.

Who gave you the Countries that you now inhabit, and by what right do you possess them?

ADARIO
HURON CHIEF

August 23

Too many of our efforts are like scrambled eggs all thrown in together, whipped and beaten and without much substance. What we do overlaps too much—sleep lets worry in, eating is not prepared but brought in with its ingredients totally beyond our knowledge. Walking has become a contest, a thing of speed and clever costumes. Talking is chatter and boastful—and prayer is too often listening to someone else who "knows how."

Whatever we choose to do should be done with all our hearts. Not done so we can feel important by running here, running there—but done in love for the sake of love, and not for competition. Who we are, what we are, where we are going and when we get there has to do with the mind and spirit more than what the Cherokee calls *nu s di da nv*—how people see us.

You can count your money . . . but only the Great Spirit can count the grains of sand and the blades of grass.

BLACKFEET

August 24

Never let another person tell you what to think and what to do. Start now to think things through and get ready for what you want. You have to be prosperous in your thinking long before you see the money. Your health must have the support of your mind and words before it can keep its good condition. You have to be lovable before anyone can love you.

We think "instant" when it takes time. Remember the flower—first the bud and then the bloom, and all the steps that go in between. What do you want? See it now in your mind, and keep on seeing it so clearly that it becomes a treasure map. Enjoy looking at it and stop questioning whether it is going to work. It is your map—give it your attention.

We talk to Wakan tanka and are sure he hears us.

CHASED-BY-BEARS
SANTEE-YANKTONAI SIOUX

August 25

We are the designers, the engineers, the builders of our lives. But we are notorious for not staying with any one of these things to complete it because we are afraid something is developing in another area that we don't know about.

Stick to it. Study it out and get so involved that nothing else can compete in importance. See each detail, measure every idea, refine and improve until you know it like the back of your hand. Be steady and consistent and never count yourself so important that you cannot stand corrected. Albert Einstein put it this way: If A equals success, then the formula is A equals X plus Y and Z, with X being work, Y play, and Z keeping your mouth shut.

For him [the old Indian] to sit upon the ground is to be able to think more deeply and to feel more keenly; he can see more clearly into the mysteries of life.

STANDING BEAR
LAKOTA

August 26

He sat easily on the ground and leaned his back against the rough bark of an oak and spoke solemnly of a problem relatively new to Cherokees. "Time was when *ka ni gv na w* that doctors call depression was not in our camp. We had our land and families, but it changed. Old ones cry to leave land and trees, children wave little hands. Hardship not new, reason new.

"A scar is depression in skin. A hurt is depression in soul. Medicine cure cuts, but only Spirit cure hurt. Speak to it in your prayer and tell it go. Refuse it a place and always say thank you. Sing some, too. Deep in soul, sing, and it iron out depression."

I am afraid that the white men are not speaking straight . . .

CHIEF WENINOCK
YAKIMA
CIRCA 1915

August 27

Guilt imagines that every eye sees and every mind judges. But guilt can be false—a thing of the conscience that becomes so real it rules our common sense.

We are aware that all guilt is not false—but for most people the fear of someone thinking we are guilty is reason enough. What we do not realize is that it is our own thinking, our own emotion and fear that keep us weaving and dodging.

A person trying to lose a few pounds feels guilty if someone sees him eating. A prudent spender feels the weight of spending a dollar—and so goes the guilt which is not guilt at all but fear. From one fear comes a thousand things to get rid of—and false guilt should be the first.

Will you sit idly by, supinely awaiting complete and abject submission, or will you die fighting?

PUSHMATAHA
SHAWNEE

August 28

Nothing and no one is worthy of sacrificing the best of oneself to please or placate. We have the right to refuse anything that would destroy our own honor or self-esteem. Right and wrong may not always be clear cut for us, but if we hold to what we know is right, we will not have failed.

Regaining self-respect may be more difficult than losing it, but it can be done. We only have to consider where we want to be a week, a month, or a year from now. Will the path we are on get us there? Sometimes the wisest thing is to turn around and go back to common sense.

Our children were never known to cry of hunger, and no stranger, red or white, was permitted to enter our lodges without finding food and rest.

BLACK HAWK
SAC

August 29

We can forgive ignorance to some degree, but willfulness is another issue. The sad part is that the two so often go hand in hand to create danger. The main objective of this personality is to take advantage, to prey on anyone or anything for no particular reason—other than because they can.

The wise thing is to be aware—to see and sense anything out of order. Don't, through compassionate thinking, give opportunity or reason to anyone, however kind and friendly they seem, to take advantage. Many have lost a great deal by being too trusting. But trust should not be passed out like calling cards—even to someone we have known before. Times have changed—and maybe the personality as well.

Had our fathers the desire, they could have crushed the intruders out of existence with the same ease we kill the blood-sucking mosquitoes.

BLACK HAWK
SAC

August 30

Regardless of how grownup we may appear, we are children at heart. We want to know what lies over the hill, what makes strange sounds, where a path leads, and what will happen if we do a certain thing.

A natural curiosity lives in all of us. It keeps us interested and inquisitive, alive and well-adjusted. Even our children think we can see around corners and find treasure—and we can.

If we could live life all over again, would we do it differently? In some areas—probably. Anyone who fails to see his own mistakes is in danger of making them again. But in most cases, it is a delight to sing and keep fear away that we have missed the most important parts of life.

My heart is good; these people do not tell the truth when they say their hearts are good.

KEOKUK
SAC AND FOX

August 31

A person totally dominated by his emotions is little different from a piece of paper lifted and tossed by the wind. Everything centers around caution—don't do this, don't say that—or an emotional explosion can take place.

None of us escape emotional extremes. We have cried our hearts out and laughed hilariously in all the wrong places. We have known melancholy and ragged nerves. But most of us know how to stabilize our feelings. The unstable times are when someone feels he has a right to blow. Without sadness or happiness we could be deadly indifferent, but to be blown about with every emotion is a waste of human spirit.

May the Lord bring you out of all your troubles. Trust your course with Him.

JEREMIAH EVARTS
ATTORNEY FOR CHEROKEES

NINE
So' nali

NUT MONTH
Dulu stinee'

AMAZING GRACE
By John Newton
Cherokee version

Ooh nay thia nah,
Hee oo way gee'
E gah gwoo yah hay ee.
Naw gwoo joe sah,
We you low say
E gah gwoo yah ho nah.

September 1

Our pride can rob us of the help we need—and the other person of the chance to do a good deed.

Why is it so hard to accept help without feeling something very close to anger? Is it because we think we have not done as well as the other person or do we feel too great for self-sufficiency?

When we need help we have not fallen short. If we have done everything we can to help ourselves then we should consider it the other person's time to give. If we are made to feel awkward for needing help, we can remember the feeling when it comes our time to help out. Pride is an admission of weakness and gratitude is a sign of strength. We can receive graciously and we can give the same way.

We should not despair of once more enjoying the blessings of peace in our new homes.

JOHN ROSS
CHEROKEE CHIEF

September 2

Everything has a reason. We may have to wait a while to understand, because much of what we see is a puzzle with all its pieces strewn about. The whole thing is there but in our present condition we do not comprehend the first thing about fitting the right pieces together. It is going to take some time.

Maybe our dullness is necessary to keep us from making foolish moves. It is better to stand and let life creep back in and our blood to flow normally before we begin again. We still do not know the reason for something but we handle the time better and we recover our senses more quickly.

We are all Seminoles here together. We want no long talk; we wish to have it short and good.

CHIEF JOHN HICKS
SEMINOLE
1829

September 3

The need for security can create an uneasy nest. Where do we go? What do we do? But the most unholy of questions is, "Where did I fail?"

Change does not mean failure. It means upheaval and it means trial and effort, but it does not mean failure. Anger about change means we have not thought it through, we have not looked beyond the limits, beyond the perimeter of what is familiar.

The biggest problem is that the ones who instigate it are not the ones that make the change. But those who make the change will eventually find it was the best thing that ever happened. It brought out new strengths and new thinking and the knowledge that security is not in other people—but in ourselves.

Day and night cannot dwell together.

SEATTLE
SUQUAMISH CHIEF

September 4

Some of us have used our minds like *u yo*—leaving the lids off the can so that it collects *u yo* which is Cherokee for garbage. No wonder we have so little self-reliance, we learn so little from our experiences.

Each of us needs to keep a close eye on everything we do. This is a whole new world without observance of many rules. We used to know what was safe and what should be watched, but the times have changed and many of the so-called rules have been rewritten.

Good things and good people still exist and we should be a part of it. But it is not wise to leave ourselves open to every passing bit of trash.

The time was when our Father, who lives above the clouds, loved our fathers, who lived long ago, and His face was bright, and He talked with our fathers.

WASHAKIE
SHOSHONE

September 5

On this long list of important things, is this present worry anywhere near the top? It could be, but most likely it isn't. In a split second fear can shuffle our priorities into a jumbled mess until we see it all as one big hurdle.

Stop and ask if this is fact or fear. Fact can even be changed, but fear has a way of taking our deepest fear and molding it into a monster. We have a flair for begging monsters to stay away when we should be calling them cowards and shriveled and gone. We have the authority to do it—and it works because words have the power of life and death!

I want to tell you this, because I believe if you know it you will correct the evil.

LITTLE RAVEN
ARAPAHO

September 6

We've known extremes. We have pushed beyond common sense and we have paid a price for it. Most of us know what is good for us, but we allowed ourselves to be influenced where we should have stood our ground.

This is true even of the little things— though often the results are not little at all. Things like eating and drinking and talking too much, these things are not bad in particular, but so easily overdone. There's no obvious stopping place so we are well past the stop sign before we know it is there. Education? Awareness? Group understanding? These things may help, but a thorough adjustment in the soul and spirit is the only lasting answer.

My Great Father . . . told me that fire and water were alike, and that we cannot live without either of them.

LONE WOLF
KIOWA

September 7

Many weak excuses come to mind to give us a right to self-pity—we don't feel well, we haven't slept in a week, or we simply don't know what others expect of us. All these things can be true and all have a devastating effect, but we could have said we are in the midst of a pity celebration.

Mind games tell us we need an excuse to keep from being overwhelmed with obligations. We don't need any excuse to say we are simply not up to the challenges at this time. If people want to be offended it is their privilege, but right now self-honesty and rest are more important.

I have no father or mother; I am alone in the world. No one cares for Cochise.

> COCHISE
> APACHE

273

September 8

Autumn shadows grow long across the land and a sunset washes the sky with colors of a ripe peach. The color deepens and spreads in cherry-colored streaks until even the grasses in the meadow are tinted pink.

A single cry from the deep woods could be the wail of a coyote or the shriek of an owl. Such primitive voices speak of sameness even while they change the human world.

Daytime activity ceases when evening draws its shadows through the woods. Deer feed quietly. Hounds pursue the raccoon and hundreds of tracks along the feed road tell us that humans may walk here but other species own the night.

We never did the white man any harm; we don't intend to.

TALL BULL
CHEYENNE

September 9

There are ways you have not dreamed existed—until you can see beyond your own limited vision to possibilities of real substance. It takes a certain mindset to stop believing in shortages and start seeing good things happen.

Some people believe they will never see their dreams fulfilled—they accept it. And that acceptance solidifies such beliefs into reality. You have developed a consciousness of *ga lu lo gi*, the Cherokee's expression of lack.

In the words of the prophet, "Is anything too hard for God?"

We are all poor men; and I think others have got all the goods.

SATANTA
KIOWA

September 10

Having a lot to think about and maintain makes us think our memory is not as good as it once was—and more than likely it isn't. Not because of age or disease of some kind, but because we hear more than we used to; we have more trying to get our attention. But the main reason we don't recall as easily is that we don't want to. We are weary of having to be on our toes with useless facts and figures.

If all the activities of daily life are important enough, we will make a way to remember. Deep thought and meditation can displace things of memory we once thought important.

Any good thing you say to me shall not be forgotten.

TEN BEARS
COMANCHE

September 11

Everything is not our fault. All of life is not our doing. But the one thing we can count on is our thinking. Think things through honestly and without excuse. Don't tell it, and don't think that's all there is to it.

The mind is the doorway to the heart and spirit. This is where the real part of us lives, where life springs forth or gives up. Knowing this, we can go in and clean house and begin to feed ourselves life-food. Life-food is from *Galun lati*, the Spirit—and without the Spirit, everything is our fault. Never be without the Spirit.

You fought me and I had to fight back.

GALL
HUNKPAPA SIOUX

September 12

If you are standing deep in trouble don't talk disparagingly of things spiritual. Spirit is your hope. It is your wisdom and your healing, key to your money and your relationships. If you believe these things are not true—then you have the reason for your emptiness.

"Prove me now," the wisdom goes. Spiritual things are provable. There is wisdom that can be tapped and put to good use when it has made the right connections. Right connections are not just people but Spirit. Breakdowns occur without Him, breakthroughs happen with Him.

We want to keep peace; will you help us?

RED CLOUD
SIOUX CHIEFTAIN

September 13

It is good to keep the promises we make to ourselves to enjoy a peaceful hour. How long has it been? How long has it been since we walked on a grassy hillside and watched the shadows hover and move?

Walking is good for the legs—but it does wonders for the soul. The autumn season is one of the best times to walk and think. There is a rhythm in the earth that rises into our feet when we walk. In it is healing and it centers the soul so that the cares of the world cannot get in to destroy peace. And peace has so many side effects. It restores youth and gives perspective to a world-weary mind.

The Great Spirit made these mountains and rivers for us, and all this land.

BLACKFOOT
CROW
1850s

September 14

All of life is not as clear-cut as we would like it. The gray areas need careful examination because they are too often taken at face value. The tendency is to make a judgment without first seeking wisdom.

The belief system is jolted when there are too few answers and too many questions. Something may be a fact but not truth. Facts waver and change—but truth is truth at every point.

We were told to know the truth and the truth will make us free. It doesn't say know the facts—because facts change. But nothing can destroy truth—and eventually it will assert itself.

I have worked with one heart, and one object.

KICKING BIRD
KIOWA

September 15

Zeal is very human. Every successful diet, every effort to think positively, and every good intention is preceded by zeal. But the results are often mixed, because without wisdom and understanding there is no power to sustain zeal—no real change inside.

Human effort without spirituality is like the grasshopper in autumn. Its desire to spring as high as it did in spring is overtaken by lethargy.

Ability is a hundred times more effective with a reasonable amount of zeal—but add wisdom and the grasshopper mentality is lost forever.

I have buried the past; and I don't want to be mad for the past.

CAPTAIN JACK
MODOC

September 16

Perception can be very wise but reading between the lines in other people's lives is only guesswork. By rationalizing and putting two and two together it can almost be assumed that something is a certain way, right? Wrong.

People identify with other people because of their likenesses—but there is nothing new under the sun. Human nature is human nature and will stay that way until we all stand close enough to the divine.

We are ever so much better served not to guess about other people. And we are better people when we mind our own business.

The Apache was unlike any other Indian Tribe the whites have ever fought.... He saw no reason for fighting unless there was something tangible and immediate to be gained.

A FRONTIER CAMPAIGN OFFICER
CIRCA 1860

September 17

We all know the difference between right and wrong. Even without teaching there is an innate knowing that reminds us when we have overstepped our right or someone else's.

Every time we prefer not to keep a law or a rule we say it was put in place to punish us. But it really says to go this way and you will be protected, like driving the right way on a one-way street. But natural laws are for our good as well. They are reflections of spiritual laws and should be revered.

Respect for ourselves and for others covers a multitude of rules. Akin to love, it saves a person from himself.

When people come to trouble it is better for both parties to come together without arms, to talk it over, and find some peaceful way to settle.

SPOTTED TAIL
SIOUX

September 18

We are conditioned to stampede. Heard the latest? Then run! Run on the inside even when your body is perfectly still. Run up your blood pressure because what you see and hear is not fair—not in keeping with what you have always believed.

Things are not always going to be the way we think they should. They never have been and they are not likely to change this week. But listen, be glad you know the difference. And be glad there are others who agree with you, but don't plan on that making a big difference in the way the world thinks. Plan to go on thinking fairness—it is the seed that will eventually produce.

Osages have talked like blackbirds in the spring.

GOVERNOR JOE
OSAGE
1800s

September 19

Eagles soar more surely than we walk—but even so we are eagles in spirit. Physical wings are not so important to us if we can free our spirits to soar.

As a symbol of freedom, the eagle builds its aery higher than any other nests and its eyes have vision that can survey anything moving far below. It sets its wings to catch the wind and its flight is graceful and beautiful. Unlike us, it takes time to renew and restore—even its beak is renewed and its old feathers replaced with new ones.

When we set our minds and spirits to do something, nothing can bring us down. But rest and renewal are necessary—and never just luxuries to be avoided.

I am here by the will of the Great Spirit, and by His will I am chief.

SITTING BULL
SIOUX

September 20

Blues are not measles that run their course. They are leeches that hang on as long as there is a tear, a groan, or a down attitude. But nothing is as subtle or determined to get you by the throat, and it is well worth the effort to get rid of them at first sign.

But how? Stop the mind from falling into uselessness that is a quagmire. When there seems to be no point to anything discouragement sets in. But it is an emotion that rocks the soul the way the wind shakes a boat. Let the weak say, "I am strong." Speak to yourself in very certain terms that this is the end of blues and the beginning of colorful thoughts and delightful days. Then put your hands to work and give your mind a rest.

The Earth-Mother is listening to me and I hope that all may be so arranged that from now on there shall be no trouble.

GERONIMO
APACHE

September 21

Put a lid on all the nonsense, the frenzied chatter, the idle conversation that gets around to criticizing—with or without reason.

Talking is like a leak in a dam. At first it is only a tiny trickle but the longer it goes the greater the flow, until it begins to gush. One comment can bring on another and another, and before we know it we have said things we never intended to say.

It is enough to know something, to feel it and think it, but to speak it opens the way for our words to be recorded forever in the atmosphere. What do we want to our credit?

It makes my heart sick when I remember all the good words and broken promises.

CHIEF JOSEPH
NEZ PERCE

September 22

As surely as lines are drawn to shut someone out—those same lines are shutting someone in. One side of the line is little different from the other, but those drawing the lines believe they are on the high side.

Most people have a greater ability to choose up sides and show disdain than they do to love. And love is the only safety zone, the only place where people can come together and show concern and get to know each other. Some believe others have no right to be anywhere—and such was the case at the Battle of Little Big Horn.

Long Hair [Custer] thought he was the greatest man in the world. Now he lies there.

WHITE BULL
SIOUX CHIEF

September 23

Other people's opinions are simply a view, not a verdict. A certain type of personality wants his view to be the effective one—the one that says what should be valid and what should be invalid. But even if he was right for the moment, does he have to be right forever?

Listen, we can change. Any of us. It is our privilege to put down the old nature and to take on the new. It will be suspect—things like that always are. But St. Paul was a rascal until he made a change one day. We can do that—and we can move out of the range of those who will not accept the change. Seems that it would be the best revenge to be good even though the skeptics raise their eyebrows.

We want to know whether you are going to fight the Sioux or not. We want to know.

BLACKFOOT
CROW

September 24

When we have a genuine interest in something we seldom lack the energy to do it. Hour after hour thought and energy flow into the routine and weariness has no part.

There will surely be some necessary work that will not excite us—but we can refuse to be dull and slow of mind and spirit.

How many times we have nearly given up because we could not see creativity or color. And then a change would come—a different view and energy would flow in and the misery would be forgotten. Energy can only flow when it is connected to a live circuit. Our work is to stay connected.

I am not talking anything badly or angrily, but simply the truth.

SATANTA
KIOWA

September 25

Don't fret. When you can affect the outcome of something toward peace, do it. But stewing about those things you can't do anything about is wasted energy.

Many of our problems would disappear if we did not keep them going with our fretting. We nag ourselves into despair and shoulder guilt that isn't ours.

No doubt we have reason to be upset, but who doesn't. The ideal solution is to love and let go. The practical answer is to keep our mouths shut and let the knots unravel. They will.

They do not work underhanded at all, but declare plainly that they want peace.

SATANTA
KIOWA

September 26

Walk with me to the edge of the woods and hear the birds. They haven't all gone south, some stay the winter. The cardinal will later perch in the evergreens and make the snow seem whiter—but now he sings in the bottomland that is protected from the wind.

See the last of summer's flowers, the sunflower that is a great deal bigger than the palm of your hand. And watch the lone jet draw lines from one horizon almost to the other before the wind scatters his lines. Even when the season seems to be taking away all that the land has produced—remember the potential is still there, and so is yours.

We gave you our hearts. You now have them.

SATANK
KIOWA

September 27

E li si said, "Lie on the earth with your feet higher than your head when you are very tired. Roll your feet to keep from making noise. No one hears you and it rests your feet."

She said, "Lonesome? Sing. When Indian sing he touch something higher than himself.

"Not feel good? Put bare feet on bare ground. Healing rise out of deep pulse of earth. Can't think? Close eyes and go to mountains in your heart. Mountains just a place but trip take you out of worried mind. High-priced medicine don't compare to natural. Reach toward sky and raise up on toes—several times. It might not help you—but who knows."

All who go through among my people may find peace when they come in.

TEN BEARS
COMANCHE

September 28

On rare occasions you may have felt a word drop into your heart that you knew meant something because it never faded and always stood as a reminder that something profound happened. You may not have understood then, but your mind has gone back to it numerous times, wondering what it meant.

Years can pass between an event and the understanding of it. It may be we have to grow up to it, or our minds and spirits have to mature enough to see how it is to play out in our lives. It is little different from building a house, you can see the structure going up, but you know it can't be used until it is finished. Sometimes ideas and visions need time to firm up before we can use them.

The designs of Providence, in the course of events, are mysterious . . .

JOHN ROSS
CHEROKEE CHIEF

September 29

Certain sounds and fragrances come through more clearly in autumn than any other time. It is always satisfying to take a thermos of coffee and a sweet roll and disappear into the countryside just to sit and absorb the unending wonders of nature.

Beneath the bent grasses in the meadow is new growth of plants that will survive the winter. Mullein that is called Indian tobacco spreads its broad furry leaves and will grow low until spring. All along the paths are wild turkey tracks and tracks that appear to be small palm prints but belong to the raccoon. Red tail hawks ride the currents overhead and a flock of gulls turn silver as they move swiftly. It is autumn, but it is even more. This is life that gives us peace.

Holy Mother Earth, the trees and all nature are witnesses to your thoughts and deeds.

WINNEBAGO WISDOM

September 30

Careless words and controversial thought can hang on the invisible like dust clouds and clog thinking and comprehension like the webs of cobbies. Personal space should be kept as clean as the plate you eat off of—and you should never open the door to heedless opinion.

The atmosphere swarms with spoken words—and most are hostile and hardened by experience. If each of us could see with the naked eye our own personal words, even without the multitudes that belong to others, we would be appalled. The computer shows what is preserved on the internet, but think what people verbally send into the ethers—and every word frozen in time.

Black Hawk is a true Indian. He feels for his wife and children, his friends . . . they will suffer. He laments their fate.

> BLACK HAWK
> SAC
> CIRCA 1800

TEN
Ska' hi

HARVEST MONTH
Duna Na Dee'

*When the future historian writes
the history of the red man of the
forest and the prairie, the name
of our great departed Sioux
Chief, Sitting Bull, will appear
among the noble characters.*

October 1

What person does not hope for a spiritual experience that will connect him with the inevitable source of all good? What person does not hope for a touch to open his stoney heart to understand his own potential? Who has not fallen prey to a mountain of misinformation and to the belief that there is no justice in the world?

While the world of events whirls and spins and shocks the rural soul, the sophisticated person of broader experience says that is the way it is, and that is why we act the way we do. But that very opinion propels a person headlong into the whirring teeth of absolute destruction. Who will hit the button? Who will stop this swift descent? It is a personal responsibility, a very personal responsibility, and who can do it?

You can dictate your terms. I am your prisoner, and must submit, but I am still a man, the same as you.

BLACK HAWK
SAC

October 2

Sweet fragrance of the land, herbs and roots and medicines long lost to the general populace, are nonetheless as present as they always have been. We have been so taken with miracle cures, these things have been put away as folklore and not dependable. The simple people at one time had no other alternative—so runs the present-day popular notion.

Hard-fought battles over who is to pay for the miracle medicines—and we are grateful for most of them—may turn a venturesome soul back to the soil and back to those things that heal a mind and body without being asked for proof of insurance. But one other thing far too ignored is the power of prayer. No Indian is remiss in blessing his body and his soul and spirit because he knows they work together. His prayer is not now and again but regular and potent.

The lack of respect for growing, living things soon led to lack of respect for humans too.

LUTHER STANDING BEAR
LAKOTA

October 3

The first crystal clear morning after days of blue mist is like music after a long silence. Even the cool air does not dampen the spirits of domestic animals and those that live in the woods.

A young bobcat in prime coat wanders along the rock ledge in full view but unaware of interested eyes. No doubt he hunts for field mice and that explains why the barn cats have stayed so close to home.

We have not felt the extremes of oncoming winter, but time will insure it. Meantime, adjust, adjust. Don't be taken by surprise. Prepare for change and the unexpected within change.

Our people possessed remarkable powers of concentration . . . and I sometimes fancy that such nearness to nature . . . keeps [us] in touch with unseen powers.

CHARLES EASTMAN, PHYSICIAN
SANTEE DAKOTA

October 4

Questioning Aunt Nellie was an eye-opener. Her face, some said, was like the wrinkled Black Hills but it was wreathed in smiles and mischief when we asked her most favorite things. She said quite simply:

"A full box of wooden matches, a jar of mentholatum, the smell of coffee . . . and I reckon any kind of fresh fruit.

"Young children were sent to neighbors to borrow fire . . . and when our legs ached *E li si* rubbed kerosene on them to warm the muscles. The other things are just something I liked and still do. No, we didn't have anything, but we knew how to hunker down until the hard times passed."

And then she added, "People need to learn how to do that now."

Say to us if you can say it, that you were sent by the Creative Power.

TOOYALAKET
NEZ PERCE

October 5

As a very small child I was in the care of my mother's teenage brother while she worked in the garden. Inventive as he was, he tied a rock to my dresstail to keep me from toddling off. Needless to say, this was not acceptable and I shouted with rage.

My fearful mother came running from the garden and scolded her brother unmercifully—so he removed the rock and I felt terrible because he had been scolded and tried to get him to tie the rock on again.

It became a family memory to laugh over—but it tells of a person's willingness to bear a burden. Are we supposed to drag a rock, bend under a heavy load, or carry the shame of something to make us stronger? Don't believe it. Look behind the rock and you won't find a caring uncle, but a deceiving idea.

I will not fall on the rocks. When I die my enemies will be under me.

CAPTAIN JACK
MODOC

October 6

Living is a little like a wedding—to make a deal takes only a minute, but to live with it may take a lifetime. Many have not learned that life is not a quick trip down the aisle and if you don't find it to your liking you can start all over again.

A good marriage is one of adjustment and then readjustment. It is sharing the hardships and the growing and sweetening that are in the middle of hardships. Little can compare with faith and looking out for others. It is giving and receiving, and we know it is not something outside ourselves that makes life worthwhile but what we have in our hearts.

I will keep my word until the stones melt.

DELSHAY
APACHE

October 7

We get to know ourselves when we are alone. What may have brought us to this place may not be as important as what to do now that we are here. When we are with other people we listen to them, but in solitude we follow our own way. Great strength comes from the quiet and it prepares us for times when the sands run very fast.

Solitude is never withdrawal but being with ourselves, learning what affects us, and what of it can be given to others. We learn how to be a good friend when our attention is not divided—a good friend to ourselves and a good friend to another who needs it.

It is hard to fight people that live like groundhogs.

TECUMSEH
SHAWNEE

October 8

St. James says to keep quiet, control your tongue—though no one ever has. Your boat may be huge, but your little tongue is a rudder that can turn a very big ship in the wrong direction. The tongue is like kindling wood that can set a whole woods on fire. Keep your tongue quiet, very quiet.

And then St. Mark says to speak—speak to the mountain and tell it to be gone. Not only be gone but sink into the sea. A mountain of trouble needs us to use our tongues. Speak what you want and need, not what you do not want.

There is a time to speak and a time to keep silence. These are the times that make us who we are, what we are, and what we will have. Life and death are in the power of the tongue.

You say you are right and we are wrong. How do you know this to be true?

RED JACKET
SENECA
1800s

October 9

Never take on more than is yours to handle. When you are a caretaker by nature, it can appear that the whole world rests on your shoulders. Some of it does, of course, because no one is without responsibility. But when you begin to think you have to do it all, it is time to back off and reassess your position.

Life is a matter of give and take—and if you try to do all the giving, someone is going to get the idea they don't have to do anything. The only way they can receive is to give first. And if someone else does all the giving, there's something amiss—and it may be you.

Our patience . . . is exhausted, and we are discouraged from persevering any longer.

JOSEPH BRANT
MOHAWK
1800s

October 10

If you argue with stupid reasoning you end up being stupid. Expressing an opinion can run you out of bounds and into areas that are not yours to argue. And no one has any business matching wits with someone who hasn't a notion of honor.

Consider what good can possibly come from a heated debate with someone who is in it for the argument alone. When there is noise and insult, the reason is weak. Someone said ignorance is behind every argument—but let's not let it be ours.

You pretty good fighter, Quanah, but you not know everything.

QUANAH PARKER
COMANCHE
1800s

October 11

Know who you are and don't worry about what other people think. Be your own best friend and resist trouble like wildfire. Be steadfast in good times and bad, tell fear to get lost and do away with doubt the way you would turn a hose on a fire.

Never fall into the habit of believing you are always in the wrong. It can be a sufferer's trap, like a wastebasket that catches all the trash. Time is precious and you don't have time to stand in a hole. Make a difference now by lifting your vision of yourself. There's no such thing as bad blood when your heart is right.

French trappers said a great many things to our fathers, which have been planted in our hearts.

CHIEF JOSEPH
NEZ PERCE

October 12

The path to the woods is soft and silent underfoot. Wet leaves pad the ground beneath the trees and bright patches of green moss cover every rock. Many plants in sheltered places thrive even now.

This place is sweet solitude—but never silent. Twittering birds have moved in for the winter and the red and blue of the cardinals and bluejays color the darkening woods. Time hangs between autumn and winter in mellow breezes and a few bright yellow sunflowers. It is a pensive time, a time to reflect and let go and enjoy.

The old Indian still sits upon the earth instead of propping himself up and away from its life-giving forces.

STANDING BEAR
LAKOTA SIOUX

October 13

Luther, a *Tsa la gi*, explained his creative God by saying, "God take Himself and make the fish, God take Himself and make the *tsi s du* [rabbit]; He take Himself and make the *wa ya* [wolf]; He take Himself and make the squirrel, and He take Himself and make me. These things my brothers."

But, Luther, what do you do when you want to go squirrel hunting?

Merriment danced in his black eyes and he added, "I just say, squirrel-brother, God made you for me!"

I traveled thousands of miles along our winding trails, through unbroken solitudes of the wild forest, listening to the songs of the woodland birds.

POKAGON
POTAWATOMI CHIEF
1833

October 14

Contentment happens when our emotions give place to common things that in other times can draw little attention. It is releasing a deep inner peace that heals sadness and lifts a sagging spirit.

Contentment is an intensely personal thing, adjusting to different people in its most effective way. It rides a shaft of sunlight to pool on the gray bark of a tree, or it rises from laughter, deep and kind. It is nearly always unexpected and settles as softly as a bird lights on a limb.

It is a remarkable fact that we simply let contentment happen. Socrates called it a natural wealth, but most have called it a miracle.

Kinship with all creatures of the earth, sky and water was a real and active principle.

CHIEF STANDING BEAR
SIOUX
1800s

October 15

Some of us go to great lengths to keep from doing detail work—anything from flipping through a directory for one name in ten thousand to guessing at amounts in a recipe. No time, no time.

Time isn't saved by guessing. Even when we hit it right once in a while—most of the time we are just a little off. How many of us take our basic instructions from hearsay—how many don't really want to know anyhow?

Life itself has an instruction book. There's no reason to guess at what is right or wrong. We have a script for every part we play in life. When we have a need of any kind, the script has the wisdom to handle it. The Scriptures leave out nothing—and the biggest mistake we can make is to say we don't believe it—and go off to figure it out by guessing.

We were put here by the Creator and these were our rights.

CHIEF WENINOCK
YAKIMA
1855

October 16

There were ducks on the pond this morning, a pair of blue-winged teals gliding smoothly along and stopping only to feed. They were oblivious to cattle feeding along the slopes—and even to footsteps on the grass. It is a calm peace of mind that is not easily startled.

Everywhere is beauty, the cottonwood tree white against the oaks and evergreens, the ungainly heron wading at the water's edge. So common and so unlikely to attract attention because it all fits together in a picture so easily taken for granted. But the peace cannot be taken for granted because it seeps into the soul like sunlight pierces the deepest shadows—and rests.

I questioned the trees and bushes . . . Who made you? In dream Wakan Tanka told me I must honor his works in nature.

BRAVE BUFFALO
SIOUX

October 17

We forget the road we have been over together . . . how difficult it was and how good. We matured together, giving courage and understanding.

Undoubted loyalty is there between us, knowing always that we can rely on kindness. We put aside anything we could not understand until it became clear.

The divine wrote in our contract to take care of this person, to load every rift with good humor and good words and always with the knowledge that we are not alone. We have planted good seeds, we have cultivated—so now comes the harvest. The joy of it is knowing we are not alone.

It is the same with human beings—there is someplace which is best adapted to each.

OKUTE
TETON SIOUX
1911

October 18

The plain and simple doorstep has tremendous value. At any time of day or night it offers the finest view, the tranquil quiet of the autumn woods and the flickering pattern of dancing leaves.

Sit here for a few moments and leaves drift down, a monarch butterfly feeds on a pot of petunias and wispy clouds show through holes in the trees' canopy. A few industrious ants are still at work around the doorstep and watching them slows the heart beat and paces the spirit.

If it were not for this doorstep, much would slip by without notice. Peace would escape us, and time would be used in ways that took all and gave nothing.

I have learned a lot from trees; sometimes about the weather, sometimes about animals, sometimes about the Great Spirit.

TATANGA MANI
STONEY

October 19

It may be that we stay in difficulty too long because of the habitual comfort of a familiar place. The ache for the old and familiar are parts of the spirit of hindrance that keeps us trying to overcome things without too much success.

A continual suggestion says that things are never going to be any different—that we can go no further and life can be no different. But it can! It can be different and it will as soon as we reject feelings of being frozen in space. Such feelings are signs that good change is in the offing and all we have to do is to walk and talk the part—and to show gratitude that the Great Spirit is ever with us.

Men must be born and reborn to belong.

CHIEF LUTHER STANDING BEAR

October 20

Every person's privilege is to stand on tiptoe and take a look over the edge. What is the edge?

A place where fear lurks and no one dares to get too close.

Many a dream has taken us up to the edge and with quaking knees to look over the immense distance between what could be and what is reality. Most people end it right there and refuse to be scared any longer.

Change is here. We can fall over the edge or we can believe in something greater than the tangible. Let go of the weak and impossible and stand in the Light that never goes out.

Let him be just and deal kindly with my people.

SEATTLE
DWAMISH CHIEF

October 21

Don't condemn yourself. Who of us have not made mistakes? No one is perfect, but we are too quick to call ourselves stupid.

We have condemned ourselves for eating—even though that is what we have to do. It's just that we eat because it is convenient, we see it, we eat it. If we can get it without having to cook it—all the better. And all the worse—because it doesn't have in it the nutrients we need and it is gone too quickly and we are not satisfied.

Laziness has overtaken our good senses. We let ourselves fall into making it easy on ourselves—and in turn we open the door to making it hard. It is a matter of choices, but not solved by self-criticism.

The ground says, "The Great Spirit has placed me here to produce all that grows on me, trees and fruit."

YOUNG CHIEF
CAYUSE

October 22

Life is a decision, a personal decision. We can stand on drifting sand and believe that whatever will be, will be, or we can stand firmly on principle that if something is wrong we can change it.

Instead of nursing pulse-taking tendencies and listening to every commercial on what is available for medical treatment, remember our instructions: Let the weak say, "I am strong."

We can become victims of temporary relief or we can separate ourselves from the hype and discover renewal that is not temporary—but eternal. Relief by the Spirit is a reality—and totally free.

This house, the home of the English, is a medicine house, and you come here to tell us lies.

SITTING BULL
SIOUX

October 23

Opportunities abound to us every day. There is an opportunity to be sick, the opportunity to argue with someone, the opportunity to be discourteous, the opportunity to believe something that is not true.

Stop thinking you have had no opportunity. You have had every chance to do many things and some of them you have received. You were led astray by thinking you could not help yourself.

We can help ourselves. By the words of our mouths, by what we say, how we think, what we believe, we help or break ourselves. Victory comes because we are consistent in saying we are well, we are strong, we are enormously happy.

They told us not to drink whiskey, yet they made it themselves and traded it to us for furs and robes.

PLENTY-COUPS
CROW

October 24

Though summer still lingers in the last of vegetables in the garden, cooler air pushes down from the north and with it the subtle changes that color sumac and woodbine with brilliant reds.

Some song birds stay during the winter, but their songs are different. This is the season of tart red apples and woodsmoke twirling through the tops of tall evergreens. It seems only yesterday that spring broke through with her wild colors and thunderstorms. And it will seem only another day until this season has passed and the woods will green once more. Use this tranquil time to rest and walk and to enjoy seeing nature in her bare bones.

The Indian, essentially an outdoor person, has no use for handkerchiefs; he was practically immune to colds, and like the animal, not addicted to spitting.

LUTHER STANDING BEAR
LAKOTA

October 25

At one time, most of us thought we knew it all, and later on, we wished we had kept quiet until we had learned something.

Discovering the depth of one thing makes us think we have tapped a reserve of wisdom and knowledge. What we really learned was how much there is left to learn.

We want to know; it is our nature. But most rebel at being taught, especially the things of the spirit. What we learn should always be carefully examined—but never with the intellect alone and always with the spirit. Life, itself, is the spirit and it should never be allowed to suffer malnutrition.

The roots of the tree of his life have not yet grasped the rock and soil.

STANDING BEAR
LAKOTA

October 26

Thank God for things that go right. Thank goodness that we come to this place more often than we realize. And thank God that we do not go to pieces when all things do not work together.

To be grateful opens the door for more to be grateful about. Nothing is set forever in one direction so that we never have to change. But change is prerequisite to balance—a feared thing that can work miracles if we use it right. Balance is an inside job—the set of our sails, our readiness, our ability to see beyond present circumstances. We make adjustments. We let go of what we cannot change. Then balance—but we have to believe in it.

Our fathers were strong, and their power was felt and acknowledged far and wide.

O-NO'-SA

October 27

Unwittingly we have been parts of broken relationships, discrimination, poverty, disease, and overbearing personalities. These things exist, and as long as someone endures it and someone does it, it will go on.

So learn why these things happen if you want to overcome them. Learn and then don't stay where they are happening, but go on to better things. This definitely can be done. Fear and helplessness are the usual reasons we stay in bad situations—but from those two things many other evils begin. Instead, say to yourself daily that you are able, you are intelligent, and you are protected. It expands your consciousness to stand up and shake off everything that has been degrading.

A single twig breaks, but the bundle of twigs is strong.

BLUE JACKET
SHAWNEE CHIEF

October 28

If you don't want to be judged harshly by other people—then don't continually condemn yourself. You have to tell people who you are, and you do it by action, by words, and by attitude. If you intend to compete with everyone, it will show in your manner.

If you believe no one likes you, they will believe there is a reason—and not like you. If you believe social status is power, you will see the day when it breaks down. Individuality is not competition, not painful separation, but sincerity and genuine caring. These things are evident—and the person that deliberately sets out to hinder someone is headed for out-and-out loneliness.

We first knew you as a feeble plant which wanted a little earth whereon to grow . . .

RED JACKET
SENECA
1792

October 29

Something new is always an exciting prospect. It can be anything that changes the face of daily life and brings it into a new pattern that makes us feel better.

Drudgery can take over our thinking and then our actions. Sticking too close to one routine and never having a change is an obvious sign we are heading for drudgery.

If renewal is to come there must be change—even if it is to walk a short distance, talk to someone out of the ordinary, and do something for someone. These things sound simplistic but if they turn our thinking to more creativity or more relaxation, it is worth doing.

I felt that I was leaving all that I had but I did not cry.

OLLOKOT
NEZ PERCE

October 30

In retrospect, we have ignored common sense in favor of doing what we wanted to do. We wish we had not done it, but we said what we wanted to say, spoke out when it would have been better to stay quiet—we have overruled our common sense.

Looking back again, when did we get off track? What little thing stung us into action? If we learn to hear the voice of wisdom we can overcome our foolishness. Wisdom never lets us down, but ignoring it will put away from us the best friend we can have.

I am tired of talk that comes to nothing.

CHIEF JOSEPH
NEZ PERCE

October 31

Few things are mind-and-spirit-adjusting like putting our hand to a job that has been waiting too long. The bigger the job, the better our concentration.

Work keeps the hands busy and frees the mind from raw nerves and injured feelings. A time to talk will come—if it is needed at all. Sometimes busy hands like walking feet can do away with things thought to be unsolvable.

Decide to do a thing that no one else can do—a specific move away from pain. It can set the wheel to turn—maybe slowly at first—but soon you'll be on top again.

If white man wants to live in peace with Indian he can live in peace.

CHIEF JOSEPH
NEZ PERCE

ELEVEN
Du

BIG TRADING MONTH
Nu Da Na 'Egwa

*Great Spirit, the council here
assembled, the aged men and
women, the strong warriors, the
women and children, unite
their voice of thanksgiving to
Thee.* Na-Ho!

IROQUOIS
THANKSGIVING
FESTIVAL

November 1

The danger point comes after a victory when we think there are no more battles. How many wars have been fought thinking this is the war that will end all wars? Even in our own private battles we cannot lie back and think we have won the right to peace.

We do need to know and remember that we are more than conquerors. It is a life promise, but we have to claim it. Other claims have taken precedence—weariness, lack, sickness—but we are conquerors, even more than conquerors. We are winners and overcomers. Believe it, because it is true, and the more we claim it, the stronger it is.

Where is our strength? In the old times we were strong.

CHIPAROPAI
YUMA

November 2

Big job? Start out in faith. Begin to work and the power to do it will come. Make the beginning, get involved, reach to do the work, and strength and inspiration will come.

If we put as much power into a job as we do worrying about it before we begin, the whole thing would move forward with ease. Showing a willingness to work, bending to it, opens the way and then the feeling of accomplishment cannot be taken away.

Taking an action is like plugging into a strength that lies dormant until we make contact. It is not just a job well done—but a personal victory.

We know that you are very strong—we have heard that you are very wise.

CORNPLANT
SENECA CHIEF

November 3

Most anything has some distortion. Living today is a little like standing in front of a trick mirror that stretches the legs to the size of sticks and puts knees where ankles should be. What is real? What can we believe?

Even nature affords some illusion. Arid desert has mirages of water standing in pools. It looks real, but approach it and it disappears.

We must be aware of illusion—of distortion, because some businesses practice it. When our own eyes squint against truth we are creating distortion. If we can't trust ourselves to recognize the truth, who can we trust?

I could cheerfully hope that those of another age and generation may not feel the effects of those oppressive measures.

GEORGE HARKINS
CHOCTAW DISTRICT CHIEF

November 4

At one time or another we have watched someone and wondered how long it would be before we reached their stage of distress. We have been made to believe that if someone in the family has had a problem that we must have it as well.

Even with our tendencies to be like someone else, we are still individuals and what we see should teach us to avoid the same pitfalls they had. More is decided in our minds and spirits than we can imagine. We have the creative power of speech, the determination and the grit to stop falling because someone else fell. Deny every thought and every suggestion that we have to be the victims of anything.

We were becoming like them, hypocrites and liars, adulturous lazy drones, all talkers, and no workers.

MA-KE-TAI-ME-SHE-KIA-KIAK
SAUK AND FOX CHIEF

November 5

Secretly, we are afraid others will see what we know is true—that we don't have what it takes. The Cherokee says we are not *u wo hi yu*—we lack confidence and we suspect others can see it. But no one can do everything—and, even if they can, they seldom do it.

What we fear, others fear. Our needs are others' needs. Our thoughts, our worries, though hidden from view, are not in the heart of just one person—but all. There's no need for a stumbling block. We may not be superhuman but we are spirit, and spirit has no limits. Spirit is not dwarfed by circumstances. It has all power and makes us worthy.

He has done nothing for which an Indian ought to be ashamed.

BLACK HAWK
SAUK AND FOX

November 6

Autumn sunshine warms the woods and brings out the elusive woodchuck to sleep on a rock slanted toward the sun. The downy woodpecker thumps on a hollow tree and a doe huffs as she slides her hooves through a carpet of autumn leaves. This is the season of mellow fruitfulness when seed fluffs drift on the breezes, and grasses colored rose and beige bend and bob.

Whether it is nature or human nature, it is a time of subtle change, a time when geese take to the southern skyways and man tries to predict the severity of winter. But back of it all is a loving Spirit who tells us to be anxious for nothing.

So why do you ask us to leave the rivers and the sun and the wind and live in houses?

PARRA-WA-SAMEN
COMANCHE WARRIOR CHIEF

November 7

Few children still have the chance to be innocent. They have been made to look like miniature adults, taught to act adult, and abused because of it.

We sympathize with abused children and say that is the way the world is, what can we do? It is an easy loophole that lets us go on our way—wishing things were different but doing nothing to make it so. This is why we have so many throwaway children. We have cut loose from our responsibility to pray.

Where did we go wrong? We made children competitive and gave them nothing for inner strength. We curled their hair and twisted their minds. They are going to learn it somewhere—so why not from us? Sadly, we haven't given them what they need because we don't have it ourselves.

Can it be that you and your children will hear that eternal song without a stricken heart?

EAGLE WING

November 8

Listen, if you do not care about yourself, who is going to? If you are not acquainted with your own spirit, who will be?

Listen, there are secrets in your heart that you have refused to hear. There is strength in your mind and in your soul that you have not used.

Who told you that you would never amount to anything? Did you say it, or did you hear it said? It is a lie. You see, Spirit is the only One that knows you. Has He said you won't make it? Never, because He knows you can. If you will only believe in yourself, if you will only take the initiative and move one step, He will move two. All you have to do is to care about yourself and your Creator.

I have nothing bad in my breast at all; everything is all right there.

SATANTA
KIOWA CHIEFTAIN

November 9

The land has taken on the look of Thanksgiving time, of fallen acorns and pecans and walnuts. Now we see the bare branches of oaks like muscled arms lifted toward the sky, and fragrant smoke settles in the valley and hangs like gauzy curtains along the river.

Southbound geese, called by the Cherokee *sa sa-u ni go di*, still put down in the open fields to feed, to flap their huge wings, and to honk. They are not the least startled by passersby. It was a time like this when Wolf George came to my grandmother's bearing a beautiful turkey for dinner. *E li si* said, "A fine turkey, good tasting. Did you raise it?" In his gruff full-blood tones he told the truth as he saw it, "No, ma'am. Saw it roosting. Got it before someone stole it."

If any white man steal our stock, I will report it openly.

SATANTA
KIOWA
1800s

November 10

For those who have a wait-and-see attitude it is more wait than see. Then they claim it is better to not expect anything than to be disappointed.

These people build the same mental images—but they see nothing. Being able to see in the spirit is as necessary as having a blueprint to build a house. The details need to be filled in, finally coming to that completed picture—so vivid and clear that it must come into being.

Anything we touch or use was first an image, an idea, in someone's mind. Seeing it and sensing it and loving it is writing an order to receive it. Mental images should never lack from a poor consciousness. Even if it seems impossible, fill it in. Ideas often have miracles of their own.

Our fathers gave us many laws, which they learned from their fathers. These laws were good.

IN-MUT-TOO-YAH-LAT-LAT
NEZ PERCE

November 11

I sat on the pine floor behind her wood range and played with my doll while she sang "Beulah Land" and made biscuits for supper. It was a comforting hour, a time of homecoming, an aroma of baking bread and laughter and sharing what happened during the day.

E li si, Grandmother, was a caretaker, a person who fed all who came through the countryside with no hope for supper and no place to sleep. She gathered in family and impressed on them the need to help each other; she asked no favors and gave of all she had. She walks in my memory as surely as she ever walked—and surely she walks with others too.

I have not forgotten what you told me, although a long time has passed. I keep it in my memory.

GERONIMO
APACHE

November 12

Misery seems to justify making someone pay—but there is sweet revenge in finding our own inner spirit can expand quickly to push out unfairness and bitterness.

Who doesn't have the right to be bitter? A hard thing to forget, a mountain to overcome—but such peace follows. Peace spreads like warm honey across a hot biscuit and permeates all the little places that capture and hold it. The heart lifts its hands in praise for relief from the darkness of bitter memories. All of us can do it—all of us must if we are to be well and have something to share. Just let it go. Life will balance the books, it always does.

While living I want to live well.

GERONIMO
CHIRACAHUA APACHE

November 13

Brilliantly colored flashing graphics, moving, walking, and yelling salespeople, and too much real-life drama makes us sigh and give thanks for a television remote control.

We forget we have another remote control right in our thinking. We can change channels—even eliminate crazy pictures that try to fix themselves in our minds. Good music helps to smooth out the wrinkles in our turbulent thinking. Wasn't it Saul that called for a musician when he needed to think or pray?

Give yourself credit for taking control—for choosing well—and watch things turn around.

Yonder sky that has wept tears of compassion upon my people for centuries untold, and that which to us appears changeless and eternal, may change.

SEATTLE
SUQUAMISH

November 14

Having a career agenda is nothing without a spiritual agenda to back it up. Good plans and good intentions are a part of getting ahead, but it's not so different from whipping up a cake and finding there's no oven to bake it in.

We are not one dimension, or two—we are three dimensions: body, mind and spirit. Only a very foolish person believes you can develop one part and ignore the others. Balance is important—perfect balance. It is the only way we do anything, because without it we fall flat on our faces. So why plan on the sky being the limit when there's no idea what the Spirit is. Cool and suave it isn't, solid as gold it is.

When we look into the history of our race, we see some green spots that are pleasing to us. We also find many things to make the heart sad.

JOHN ROSS
CHEROKEE CHIEF

November 15

Walking in a garden is little different from walking into a room full of people. Color, shape, size, all play a part—and the more varied, the greater the interest.

Only a few dominate the garden, and they are not always the prettiest. Some are herbs and serve as good medicine, while others stand in pretty little groups and dance in the breezes.

Each of us is a part of the garden. Do we add or detract? Are we fragrant and do we require sunlight or can we survive in the shade? Do we need constant attention or are we perennial—faithful to our place and doing our best to bloom?

Two branches of the ancient Cherokee family . . . it has become essential to the general welfare that a union should be formed.

SEQUOYAH
CHEROKEE TALKING LEAVES

November 16

Things have a way of growing out of bounds in the dark of thought. But we can control them by easing them out gently, the way steam escapes the kettle. The worst thing is to feed more fuel into our emotions than we can handle. Turn off the heat and the pressure will ease.

Lay blame aside—especially self-blame. You can't do any good if you are dwelling on what went wrong. Forgive yourself and others. Nothing removes the blocks like forgiving. This is survival time and no injustice should be harbored. Make a new beginning and don't stop until it is done. You will know when that is.

The Great Spirit has heard me, and he knows I have spoken the truth.

KEOKUK
SAC AND FOX

November 17

Once we have been afraid of something it is never hard to be afraid of it again. The memory hangs in the back of the mind the way an insect can get caught in a swinging fragment of spider web. Although the same experience may not come again, even its possibility is terrorizing.

Fear is our most common emotion. It is the magician's stick that stirs the bubbling brew of all our negative feelings. Somewhere in our growing up years we learned to hide our deepest fears—but now and again we find them all over again.

Action, doing something constructive, meets fear on the darkest path and does not flinch. We give life a quiet balance when we say to fear, "You are not acceptable. I am in control and I choose freedom."

It behooves you to learn well what you are taught here.

SITTING BULL
SIOUX

November 18

Never be so bent to certain beliefs that it is impossible to see the little things that make life so much sweeter. Sure, you're going to have to deal with things—that's life. But if you don't get down in it and lose your overall perspective, you'll make short order of the work.

When you love other people you listen to their problems and offer them help, but you don't take their responsibility. You just help. Mothers and grandmothers have always had the tendency to take the whole burden, but you shouldn't. Children have to learn there is help—but some of it comes from them.

Now many things have happened that are not your fault.

GALL
SIOUX

November 19

It is lovely to think of you when leaves and grasses are all shades of chrysanthemums and sunshine is golden through the autumn haze.

It is soothing to remember you when all is quiet at the midnight hour, when it is velvet or bathed in silver.

It is comforting to know your faith overcomes your fears, that peace permeates your whole existence. You are aware that nothing equals the peace that passes all understanding.

It is with gratitude I know you are wise beyond human comprehension—and kind, even when there is reason not to be. You are the Great Spirit, the endless, loving Presence that blesses us in every hour.

The Creator ordained that people should live to an old age.

HANDSOME LAKE
SENECA
1800s

November 20

Always take into account what your mind has in it. What of the world have you taken in and stored in all the little crevices and avenues of your mind and thinking?

Guard your mind, for out of it comes what you think is possible for you. If you have stored defeat and rejection, those are the only things you have to draw on.

Our voices record everything we say within our minds and hearts. Blessing or swear words, sarcasm or snappy cynicism, all are there, and all have a part in ruling life. This is the hardest part to sweep out and control, but it can be done—and it is better than storing trash.

Neither anger nor fury shall be found lodging in their minds.

IROQUOIS
CIRCA 1570

352

November 21

Never say to yourself, "This may not work." Give support to whatever you try. You see, it hears you. It accepts your decision even before you begin.

Always tell your work that it is good and that it will serve a purpose long after it is finished. To tell it anything else is calling it by unseemly names, names that oppose its good success.

Call life by its beautiful names. Tell it how strong and honorable and good it is. It is your life and your voice, and you have the right to use them together for every good purpose.

There was never a question as to the supremacy of an evil power over and above the power of good.

STANDING BEAR
SIOUX

November 22

Don't let the night make you afraid. As children, our *e li si* (grandmother) was conservative with oil for lamps and it was a joyful time when family and friends gathered on the porch or sat on the grass and told stories after night. It was not uncommon to hear the high whine of mosquitoes. "Smudges" or small fires were laid to smoke a lot and keep the mosquitoes at bay.

Someone told snake stories or ghost stories, someone sang, someone related funny tales— but the night made it possible. Shy visitors were secure; the caring and kinship melded friendships together and children finally fell asleep on comfortable laps. Neighbors drifted away; they would happily come again—when it was night.

Give us wisdom to guide us on the path of truth.

SOSE-HA-WA
SENECA

November 23

Saying is claiming and claiming is putting a brand on something—not so different from the rancher that brands his cattle.

Be careful what you claim as your own, because you will get it whether it is good for you or not. Old decrepit age is claimed by more people than anything else. They listen to advertising and medical reports and believe they are supposed to begin giving up when they are just past forty.

Many things "could" happen, as the reporters say, but not if we stop claiming we are susceptible to every passing germ and every aging day. Speak the word and know it is right for us to brand our cattle any way we see fit—the very best, the very best.

Our old chiefs thought to show their friendship and good will, when they allowed this dangerous snake into our midst . . .

MAHPIUA LUTA
OGLALA SIOUX
1800s

November 24

It is your life, so get it all together. Go back and see where you dropped the threads you were weaving. Was there a weak one? Did it break, or was it inferior from the beginning?

Know these things. Know what happened and if it was your fault or if you tried to weave alien threads into your life. Never be afraid to admit fault, it is one of the most freeing things you can do. Simply say, "I did wrong and I am sorry. From this day on I do right"—and begin again.

Unite your effort with your new vision and don't get lazy. Get it together—body, mind, and spirit—if you want a good life.

It has come to me as through the bushes that you are not yet all united; take time and become united . . .

BIG BEAR
CREE
1884

November 25

Agreement is a power tool in getting things done. It has been written that where two agree as touching anything on earth—it will happen. This can explain why some things happen and others do not.

It is not often that we set out to agree with someone. More often we want to put our point across and we're not set to hear what someone else thinks is good. But this is one of the spiritual laws that govern a person's ability to live well on this earth.

When you have a need, or there is something important that needs to happen, call in your agreement partner and make a pact. This is the *gi ga*, the covenant between two people that produces results.

At times we did not get enough to eat and we were not allowed to hunt.

CRAZY HORSE
SIOUX WAR CHIEF
1877

November 26

The *Tsa la gi* (Cherokee) senses change. He doesn't take it from the world nor does he hear it from a voice that comes from a man. But when he stands by the flowing stream with arms outstretched, the voices speak.

The wind has lifted high above, barely touching the limbs of autumn trees, but it has in it a voice that calls us to be ready for change. It is not an imagined thing, not a lower-spirit voice, but a true message from the Great Spirit to stop looking at hardship and fear, to prepare.

A spirit of firmness comes in this call, but it is sweetness as well—a sweetness that heals all the wounds of centuries. It asks all the people to stand together in the true sense, and then they will never fail.

Remember! I have warned you to beware . . .

PACHGANTSCHILHILAS
DELAWARE
1700s

November 27

Those who have always been self-sufficient find it going against the grain to accept help from someone else. They have become the caretakers and giving over that responsibility is clearly unacceptable.

But they can come to realize that leaning on someone else can be a sign of strength. Not everyone can do it—not everyone is willing.

It takes a special strength to ask for help. But who knows what part this plays in the healing process. A time can come to show kindness and to be cooperative and to make it easy on someone else. This may be the proving time—the time that gives us a new understanding and compassion.

My brothers, a power which I cannot resist crowds me down the ground. I need help.

CHIEF STANDINGBEAR
PONCA

November 28

Cold wind and mist have pushed in to dampen the spirits of grownups—but not the children. These natural things are a part of their enjoyment during a Thanksgiving celebration.

The woods ring with voices and the sound of sword fights as rotten sticks collide in mid-air. No real duel could be this exciting or cause so many to roll in the leaves or to hide behind the gnarled wild rose.

Evening brings a rush of feet. Coyotes have set up their evening concert and the horned owl has squawled enough to impress them that it must be suppertime beside the fire. It has been a good day and something to remember thankfully.

I tell you my people, and I believe it, it is not wrong for us to get this food.

CHIEF WENINOCK
YAKIMA

November 29

Too much looking back robs us of our natural ability to change things. We are too good at finding reasons for failing, too well trained in using logic to work out our knotty decisions.

Every thinking, praying human being has access to supernatural answers to his problems, but he cannot use only human reason. And more than anything he must not give excuses or blame others for his own mistakes. Nor can we say that if we sit still long enough a miracle will happen. We have to use our minds and our hearts and our spirits—but we must also obey the rules.

Some of us seem to have a peculiar intuition.

OHIYESA
SANTEE DAKOTA

November 30

Lack of wisdom makes us believe we are destined to go through certain experiences. You can hear it in voices when we say, "It runs in the family."

The thing that runs most in the family is the mouth—the need to warn and warn and show fear and tell everyone we have bad blood. There is no bad blood that Spirit cannot fix. There is no ailment that is above His name. There is only hard-headedness on people's part to learn about it.

If someone in your family had a magic recipe, you'd be conniving to get it. Think of all you could do, think what miracles you could perform. Yet, you have a spiritual gift that is idle—when it could be your greatest miracle.

They brought their accursed fire-water to our village, making wolves of our warriors . . . and when we protested and destroyed their bad spirits, they came in multitudes on horse back . . .

BLACK HAWK
SAC
1700s

TWELVE
Tali Du'

SNOW MONTH
U Ski' Ya

*Twelve times the trees have
dropped their leaves and yet we
have received no land.*

CHIEF COBB
CHOCTAW
1843

December 1

Distant hills are blue-gray humps along the horizon and a blend of orange and purple sprays across the sky in extra-long pointed fingers. Millions of bare tree limbs give the appearance of gray fur laid across the valley.

It is winter and the first snows have dusted the woodland and sparkle on the rocks and along the trickling stream. There is a quietness here, a muted sound of dogs barking and an owl tuning up for the evening.

Now is the time for honest reflection, time to leave the gritty and unseemly, to make a new beginning. Time is of the essence. Find the new path, raise the new hope, lift up your voice in thanksgiving. This is your opportunity.

I desire you would open and clear your eyes.

TEEDYUSCUNG
DELAWARE
1760

December 2

Some of our greatest victories come when they are least expected and from sources that we have the least faith in. If the most beat-down person keeps the faith and moves ahead just as though he has a written contract with success, he will, even to his own amazement, come out a winner!

Most people think there's not a chance of success without great publicity and promotion—and the right connections. But the best connections are spiritually motivated by faith and caring that far overshadow puny human efforts. The will to win is important—but the Almighty Hand never has a failure.

The Great Spirit whispers in my ear!

BLACK HAWK
SAC

December 3

Much has grieved us, we cannot deny it. Strong as we are, believing as we do, we are still grieved, and we must overcome it.

To stop grieving does not mean we no longer care, but that we cannot let this emotion consume us when we need a steady hand and a firm step. It will creep back in unlikely moments to make us cry but time will replace the pain with happy memories.

Once we have a flicker of light we can know that grieving is at an end. It can no longer take our whole thought because we have things to do, places to go, and a life to live. This is the time.

He orders all things, and He has given us a fine day.

RED JACKET
SENECA

December 4

Early December has rich earthy color that stands for strength and durability. Hundred-year-old oaks stand guard over a multitude of younger growth and bear the brunt of cold winds and heavy snows. The little creeks hollow out from rushing waters and refill with sand and stones washed down from the hills.

Everywhere are signs of longevity and power. Huge boulders tilted on end or covered by moss and lichen harbor the fox and possum. Regardless of how cultivated the land may be in one season, it returns to nature in another. No time shows nature's raw strength like winter—and few things have to be hardier than people.

The Great Spirit and giver of light . . . has made the earth and everything in it . . .

PONTIAC
DELAWARE

December 5

The Cherokee calls this month *U Ski'Ya*—the Snow Month. A dusting of snow softens the rustling leaves and defines the edges of rocks and trees that are hidden in heavy foliage in other seasons. This is the quiet time, the sharp edge of winter adjusting the land unto itself.

The woods would be gray if it were not for the blue mist that hangs like soft gauze drapery through every glen and cleft in the hills. Evergreens thrive in soft leaf-matted ravines, and cottonwoods stand stark against the dark woods.

When the winds lay down in late evening the horizon clears to show vivid colors and every window is gilded gold until the sun disappears and the blue hour comes. It is as quiet as when the earth was created—and then an owl calls.

I stand here upon this great plain with the broad sunlight pouring down upon it. We shall be brothers and friends for all our lives.

RED CLOUD
OGLALA SIOUX

December 6

My child, know that you do not follow in the ways of those who experiment in danger. The Great Spirit has given you a mind of your own and it is a good mind, a straight mind, with strengths and vision sacred to you.

When your equals jeer and rag and call you a coward, reach down deep in your own mind and know you have gifts and power they will never know about. Never try to explain yourself, but be an example of what you have been taught. Remember if anyone, including an elder, has led you to believe a lie, that you have another Teacher that cannot lie. Hear that voice and listen well. It is grace to you and it will not let you fail.

When you say, "Fight!" we shall fight. When you say, "Make peace," we will make peace.

FOUR HORNS
SIOUX

December 7

She woke me at midnight to see the pink snow that lay on the ground—the only time I ever recall seeing aurora borealis, the northern lights playing in the far northern skies and tinting the snow.

She called me to sit beside her on the doorstep to watch the evening star nestled in the crest of a new moon. It was the only time I ever remember such a thing happening.

She got off of her horse on a rocky hill near the creek and said simply, "The horses are snorting. A rattlesnake must be nearby." It was coiled and ready to strike—but she showed no fear. She took aim with a rock and we dragged it home on a rope for others in the family to see the rattles.

She was an artist in her heart, a teacher, but most of all my loving mother.

I had a dream . . . one small round stone appeared to me that the maker of all was Wakan Tanka.

BRAVE BUFFALO
SIOUX

December 8

Elegant is the word for gulls flying overhead. Their graceful movements and backswept wings showed only black and silver as they glinted in the sun. They swooped and darted and flew in wide circles over the meadows as they fed on high-flying insects in the mellow sunlight.

Gulls in flight show the simplicity that living should have. Though they are very swift, they appear not to hurry; they go silently and they do not quarrel with each other. A person can say, "I want to be like that"—to have a purpose and to go about it without ruffled feathers and demanding attention for all the wrong reasons.

All living creatures and all plants are a benefit to something.

SHOOTER
TETON SIOUX

December 9

When the first snowflakes catch on leafless trees and crisp cold wind sweeps our faces, we know winter is in earnest. It turns the bright green canes of the wild rose to gray and sprinkles hickory nuts and walnuts on the path to the woods.

The entire landscape seems to be one color—but the variation is so subtle and low-key that it takes a little while to see the green lichen and the misty blue haze that hangs over the tiny stream.

Life sometimes appears to be at a standstill, and nothing is beautiful—no color, no shape, no hope. But if we refocus, if we are sincere and we use wisdom, we will move toward a new spring, just as does the season.

Whatever the fate of other Indians, the Iroquois might still have been a nation.

WA-O-WO-WA-NO-ONK
CAYUA CHIEF

December 10

A great loneliness falls on some people at this time of year. They feel the holidays are not for them—but for the happy people. But what they do not know is that the happy people could be like they, themselves, are if they would let it happen.

Everyone has something to handle, something that hurts down deep, but it would be wrong to give in to the spirit of loneliness or grief. This is something trying to steal our peace of mind and we are not going to let it happen.

When loneliness and melancholy knock on the door, take up the welcome mat and determine never to let them in again.

The white man is still troubled with primitive fears.

LUTHER STANDING BEAR
CHIEF

December 11

When peace is scattered, imagine a flock of gentle sheep and lambs feeding in sunny meadows. Their slow gentle gait across the slopes and among the grasses is so peaceful that the whole atmosphere is laced with serenity.

And then think what it is when a few goats get in with the sheep. Mischief begins. It is not the nature of goats to graze peacefully. They move among the sheep causing restlessness until the whole flock is ill at ease.

There are goats among us. They cry and nip and bite, they stir up activity that is not congenial, and it is a real job to separate the sheep from the goats. And more than this, we have to make sure we are not one of the goats.

Selfhood is ever calm and unshaken by the storms of existence.

OHIYESA

December 12

Winter sunsets cut through the dense woods and light them with a thousand blazing candles. The brilliance of the last rays reaches long fingers over the dark horizon to glaze rooftops with orange and to color chimney smoke.

Down along the timberline a couple of does paw the crusty snow and leaves in search of acorns. Excited coyote pups yip at the sight of their mother and a screech owl's voice quavers in the cold crisp air.

It is hard to be weary, hard to be angry, hard to be full of self when the land offers such peace. To see and hear natural things makes a huge adjustment seem as though it is so simple—and it is.

We were contented to let things remain as the Great Spirit made them.

CHIEF JOSEPH
NEZ PERCE

December 13

If there is no one else in the whole world around you, celebrate this season. Never say there is no use in decorating for Christmas when you are alone. But it is the best of reasons—you. You are as important to the Lord as anyone else on earth.

If you have to, buy and giftwrap your own present and put it under the tree. Don't wait for someone else to guess what you want—you do it. Keep the savory aromas of home cooking in your own kitchen, set the table and eat from a china plate.

This is a special time, so be a special part of it—music and all. If you are a joy to be with, you won't be alone.

Have I any apology to make for loving the Indians?
The Indians have always loved me.

GEORGE CATLIN
ARTIST

December 14

If a person is unhappy with himself, he is going to cause others to be unhappy as well. His house is divided against itself—and so it can't stand, and it makes him more unhappy.

It is said that every time someone does something wrong, someone sacrifices. It almost seems the innocent have to pay because the guilty will not accept the responsibility.

And so the time comes when we stand back and let the irresponsible put down their feet. As long as someone stands for them, they will not learn to stand for themselves. The greatest gift we can give such people is to let them alone—let them find their standing place.

We should be better pleased with beholding the good effects of these doctrines in your own practices than with hearing you talk about them.

OLD TASSEL
CHEROKEE
1777

December 15

Sit here with me and listen to the woods. Did you know the trees can talk? They do. They tell me all sorts of tales, for most have been here several hundred years and they have seen such things that we can't even imagine.

Yes, they have spoken of the wild animals, the strange ones and they have seen the things that made the huge boulders tumble from the ground. They have seen the floods that left these shells buried in the earth. And they can tell of people—your own ancestors.

But others, too, drovers with herds of cattle, outlaws and hunters, devious men hiding their cache. Some have left carvings on the stone. Put your arms around that tree as far as you can reach and listen . . . what do you hear?

Holy Mother Earth, the trees and all nature, are witnesses of your thoughts and deeds.

A WINNEBAGO WISE SAYING

December 16

Like anything else, if one is prepared to meet winter rather than cower at the thought, it is an excellent time to be happy and alive.

When we are warm on the inside and we have no excessive fears, we can lean into the wind and pace ourselves to breathe the cold air and taste the snow without absorbing it. We were created to take dominion over these things and it is time we proved it.

But as long as there is one other person who is not warm, who does not see beauty, we can't be too comfortable nor immune to winter.

I will ask him [the white man] to understand his ways, then I will prepare the way for my children.

MANY HORSES
OGLALA SIOUX
1890

December 17

Something very special happens in a Christmas sky. The heavens are deeper, bluer, and even the stars glitter electricity and energy. The sky is alive and set apart from earthly activity—reflecting so much that we know in our hearts.

But doubt and pain would steal this tranquil vision if we were to allow it. To stand and look into a Christmas sky tells us something about a Power far beyond our most vivid imagination. It removes us from competition, takes us out of pettiness and drains away the bitterness.

Listen, this is no common phenomenon, this is all life, this is all peace, this is joy unspeakable!

But if the vision was true and mighty, it is true and mighty yet.

BLACK ELK
LAKOTA

December 18

I watched her in the woods circling a red cedar not much taller than she was. It was her gift back to the woods that had given her so much peace and comfort—even when life outside the woods could be trying.

She laid garlands of popcorn and cranberries over the sturdy limbs along with burr acorns and suet in mesh bags. Scattered beneath the tree were sunflower seeds and millet that cardinals and titmice would soon clean up. But one added gift would attract unusual guests—miniature marshmallows were scattered in and around the tree, a sweet touch for woodland friends. A sweet touch, the best part of the gift. She gave, and peace would be given back to her.

Sometimes we prayed in silence; sometimes each one prayed aloud; sometimes an aged person prayed for all of us.

GERONIMO
APACHE

December 19

The road winds along the edge of the woodland and down over a steep hill until it reaches a gradual decline to the riverbottom. The land is rich with wildlife—turkeys, rockchucks, squirrels—and in the nighttime this is a meeting place for singing coyotes. Herds of whitetail feed on rich bottom grass, and mountain lions stalk their prey.

A little country school was once nestled in the glen and its storm cellar and spring still jut from the overgrown soil. Nearby a wagon road dug deep by many wheels goes on down to cross the river to join community with community. Who were these people, what were their dreams, and how did they overcome all the obstacles? They knew nothing of television or nuclear plants or miracle medicines. Some of them handled life with faith—and so can we.

We thank thee that thy wisdom has always provided.

SOSE-HA-WA
SENECA
1851

December 20

We view life with our hearts—and if someone does not have it in his heart to see something very beautiful, he will see only the hardship and distrust.

Two people in nearly identical circumstances can wake up to the same news, the same information, the same landscape—and see it in totally different ways.

One expects trouble to pass—and gives it time. The other sees problems pouring in faster than she can solve them. One sings, the other cries. We have to check our reactions and then check our hearts for corrected vision. This is our privilege—this is life meeting our expectations.

We took an oath not to do anything wrong to each other or to scheme against each other.

GERONIMO
CHIRICAHUA APACHE

December 21

Rebellion rises in us when one of our customs has to be changed. We think even when times were not easy, bits and pieces meant something to us. Leaving it behind means a little of us must stay as well.

Familiar memories can be treacherous. They grip the spirit and tell us we are losing something that cannot be replaced. But therein lies the fallacy. We do not replace what has been dear to us. We fold it in love and put it in safekeeping—while we add something new that has a place of its own. One thing does not have to pay the price for the other. Knowing this, we love what was, and enjoy what is.

Let us both own this place and enjoy in common the advantages it affords.

LITTLE TURTLE
MIAMI
1700s

December 22

Right now the season is at high glitter. Christmas trees in the square are covered with twinkling lights and shops and eating places teem with people in a holiday mood. Gifts of love and obligatory gifts pass from hand to hand and most lay their differences aside for a short time.

A time is recalled when the love and happiness were poured into our little homespun Christmas tree, and I wished for lights. My little Cherokee *u ni tsi*, Mother, took me to the doorway and pointed at the heavens so aglitter with stars. She stood quite still for a few seconds and then smiled at me and said, "It kind of puts a light bulb to shame, doesn't it?"

. . . Ere you change conditions that have brought peace and happiness.

PUSHMATAHA
CHOCTAW
1700s

December 23

Great and wonderful gifts have poured in over the years to enrich and strengthen life. A piece of plaster board painted and set outside to dry before it could be used as a blackboard, was found by the cow and she nibbled off the corner in search of salt. It worked out all right, because the paint made slick spots where the chalk would not work.

And on cold winter mornings around the holidays Grandmother *E li si* would skim the frozen cream that rose to the top of a crock of milk. A little sugar turned it into ice cream that was delicious, even in the coldest weather. The weather was cold and the snow was so deep I was told that Santa might not come through for a few days. But when the school bus made it to deliver the neighbor children they stopped at our house. On Christmas morning I had a doll with red hair and eyes that opened and closed. Love always triumphs.

Cultivate peace at home.

PETALESHARO
PAWNEE

December 24

O Lord, on the eve of Your birth, may all things and all humanity bow their knees to the gifts You have given and are still giving. Nothing has ever compared to what is ours through Your giving.

We ask one other gift, that those who suffer and those who are bitter and unforgiving will know how to get past the seeming irony of this time and claim their greatest gift. It is not meant to go to waste—not meant to be withheld.

Better than diamonds, better than gold, better than high success, this gift of life is in the throes of change. Our privilege is to change with it, to know all the mysteries—not for the sake of mystery but for its purpose, to heal, to restore, to preserve.

I see before me men of age and dignity . . . men of good judgment and consider well what they do.

SPOTTED TAIL
SIOUX
1700s

December 25

If I could lay before you the dearest gift this morning, it would be a time of no beginning and no end. It would be life filled with good health and peace and inner joy that can only come from the Spirit.

You would quietly refine your thoughts and words so that you never draw to you anything but the finest. You would rest deeply and breathe in sweet peace. You would know the tremendous difference between the material and the spiritual—turning from anger and frustration to a safe haven of love.

You would always be the most loyal friend—not to me but to yourself. All the issues of life rise out of the heart—so this is a gift from heart to heart.

I have expressed my heart to you. I have nothing to take back.

CHIEF JOSEPH
NEZ PERCE

December 26

Early winter mornings have a special quality, a clarity where long thin shadows and ice crystals in emerald and topaz lie on the grasses.

With the exception of a chortling blue jay there is little noise—as though everything bedded down last night and is reluctant to come out. A red tail hawk in search of breakfast rides the air currents far overhead where it can spot anything moving. It is strange that nature pays so little attention to what we think is beautiful in their domain—but it is equally strange that we are so oblivious to the supernatural that waits on us to recognize it.

The Great Spirit is our father, but the earth is our mother. She nourishes us, and what we put into the ground, she returns to us.

BEDAGI
WABANAKI
1900

December 27

See with the bright light of your heart, and don't turn eyes to the dark. It is there, but don't make eye contact or it will follow you home. Turn away from the sludgy, dirty, dark blue-black that makes up most of what we hear and see. Don't think you have to take it in because you have to work to live—and to work you must take on some of the cheetah's spots.

When sad eyes and performance voices turn to you and tell you that you must accept what is wrong, that you must have compassion, ask, "For what?" If someone wants to go to hell in a hand basket, there's not much you can do—but never be guilty of telling that person he can't help himself. The Great Spirit never made him that way.

I have been in a great many councils, but I'm no wiser.

TOO-HOOL-HOOL-SUIT
NEZ PERCE

December 28

Never turn your good successful idea into an organization and set up councils and committees to run it. If you do, you will lose the common touch and the organization will turn to catchy phrases and initials that identify it. Committees will spend their time having lunch and talking about promotion rather than quality.

People lose sight of quality and service as they try to squeeze out more hours, more money, more product that no longer is what it once was. Watch out for titles and power and wretched little people who want recognition with as little work as possible.

Come down off of it. Do good service, make a good product that is not chicken soup from chemical flavorings. Do everything with the motto, "I can be trusted." It will amaze you what it can do.

General Howard said, "Shut up! The law says you go on the reservation to live, and I want you to do so."

December 29

A very long time ago, among the pages of words written by ancient men is a phrase so potent it still works today. It says, "Call the things that be not as though they were."

So life is hard and scary and you have messed up miserably. Then change it by saying what you do want—by calling into being the way you want things and circumstances to be. Your words have power. They create. They shape. They call into being what you want.

You have been digging in your heels and declaring that nothing can be saved. Don't you know you are doing it? Cancel everything negative you have ever said—be truly sorry for it. And then take hold of your tongue and demand it speak right.

You propose to give us land where we can live in quiet. I accept your proposal.

LITTLE RAVEN
ARAPAHO

December 30

We move now toward a new year, a time that draws nearer the Millenium. It gives reason to think who we are and what we are about. Do we reach eagerly toward the future or does it frighten us with its weapons and voices and anger?

Think long and hard about this, for it reveals your state of existence. A person cannot go on thinking "some day" and change anything. But to say that this day is the day to make changes and to bring one's own personal spirit into alignment, that is an accomplishment.

Some feel they are not good enough to be any different. But what they don't realize is that making the effort to change makes them good enough. A person can't get there until he takes an action.

Some of our people have gone from here in order that they may have a change.

SPOTTED TAIL
SIOUX

December 31

A feast is a huge banquet of wonderful foods and wonderful friends to share it. It is a time when people honor people—and many memories are laid aside for this celebration.

But another kind of feast is in the heart—at the core where life is decided. It is the human way to believe himself victim of many things, and he starves at his center. He worries excessively about who will take care of him and who will feed him and if he will survive at all.

Never start a day without gratitude—without an inner singing of "Praise God from whom all blessings flow!" Never start a day being sour and hard to get along with. Never talk trouble nor give credence to those who do. Never give another person reason to be unhappy . . . and remember, this is your day. This is a day of celebrating new life and purpose.

On the other side of the river there is plenty of buffalo. When we are poor we will tell you.

BLACKFOOT
MOUNTAIN CROW

INDEX OF NAMES

Notes on the Native American motifs in
A Cherokee Feast of Days, Volume II

page 1: Ute beadwork design embroidered on hide. The symbolism in Plains beadwork was according to the fancy of the maker.

page 35: a Kwakiutl killer whale crest composed of appliqué, pearl and buttons on a 20th-century blanket.

page 65: Mississippian culture incised pottery, ca. 800–1700, Arkansas.

page 99: Kaska (Great Lakes) moosehair embroidery design with realistic floral motifs.

page 131: Northeast Coast double curve and plant beadwork motif, ca. 1700–1900.

page 165: insect design from Membres pottery, ca. 800–1200, New Mexico and Arizona.

page 197: Menomini (Great Lakes) beadwork design.

page 231: Pueblo flower design.

page 265: Navajo dry design. Dry, or sand, painting is associated with Navajo curing ceremonies

page 297: Zuni leaf and butterfly pottery design, ca.1870, Zuni Pueblo, New Mexico.

page 331: Zuni helix pottery design, ca. 1850–1880, Zuni Pueblo, New Mexico.

page 363: Cochiti black on white pottery bird and flower design, ca. 1800–1900, Cochiti Pueblo, New Mexico.